Praise for *Discovering the Club*

"In her new book, *Discovering the Club*, Cynthia L. Clack, J.D., a family law attorney, uncovers many truths that most people are unaware of regarding child abuse in our world today through her documented cases. Cynthia will make you aware of things you never knew before, and she will make you think twice about what you read about and hear in the media. Cynthia's knowledge of the judicial system will bring to light many truths and falsifications in reality in today's world."

—**Kathryn Raaker,** author, TV and radio host

DISCOVERING THE CLUB

PIECING TOGETHER THE PUZZLING NETWORK OF PARENTAL PIMPING, RITUALISTIC ABUSE, AND SEX TRAFFICKING

CYNTHIA L. CLACK, J.D.

Foreword by Gina Keating

RIVER GROVE
BOOKS

The names and identifying characteristics of persons referenced in this book, as well as identifying events and places, have been changed to protect the privacy of the individuals and their families.

Scripture quotations are from New Revised Standard Version Bible, copyright © 1989 National Council of the Churches of Christ in the United States of America. Used by permission. All rights reserved worldwide

Published by River Grove Books
Austin, TX
www.rivergrovebooks.com

Distributed by River Grove Books

Design and composition by Greenleaf Book Group and Carlos Esparza
Cover design by Greenleaf Book Group and Carlos Esparza

Publisher's Cataloging-in-Publication data is available.

Print ISBN: 978-1-966629-77-1

eBook ISBN: 978-1-966629-78-8

First Edition

He has told you, O mortal, what is good;
and what does the Lord require of you
but to do justice, and to love kindness,
and to walk humbly with your God.

Micah 6:8 (NRSV)

AUTHOR'S NOTE

Over the past thirty years, I have noticed an alarming uptick in the number of cases in my family law practice that pertain to the sexual abuse of children, child sex trafficking, promotion of prostitution (both child and adult), and child pornography. I have taken on cases against the predators who committed and encouraged these crimes and the "system" that too often seems to protect these predators, whether actively, by returning the children back to their abusers, or more passively, by ignoring the circumstances and looking the other way.

These stories are shocking, harsh, horrifying, and hard to believe. As you read them, you may wonder how a West Texas family law attorney could have encountered such a network of organized criminal evil that so few people openly acknowledge. It is a question I still ask myself after all these years.

The book you are holding in your hands is structured more like a jigsaw puzzle, with each chapter providing an important piece of a larger puzzle that spans the last thirty years of my forty-eight-year career as a lawyer. Just like I began to notice patterns while working on these cases, while you are reading, you may start to notice the puzzle pieces interlocking to show you a much bigger picture. When connected, these pieces begin to demonstrate the breadth and depth of the horrific abuse perpetuated by a system that sometimes turns a blind eye, denying justice for the victims and their families.

This book has no clear ending, and that is by design. I made a strategic decision to take this "unfinished" approach for a few reasons. Some of these cases are still in open, continuing litigation. Others are inactive or closed cases. However, even when the litigation comes to an end, the survivors are left to navigate the trauma, fear, and shame of their experiences for the rest of their lives.

This book is a call for justice for the victims of sexual predators. It is a call for people of integrity and courage to become aware of what is going on and to join the movement to change the way we understand and deal with child sexual abuse. There will be people who read this book who have been sexually abused who thought no one would listen to or believe them, while others may read this book and take note of how the judicial system in their own communities operates with regard to victims of sexual abuse.

As an attorney, justice is my passion and purpose. My heart goes out to the children who are victims of sexual abuse and sex trafficking and the adults who are victims of this present-day form of slavery. To those parents and adults who are trying their best to report, speak out, and shine the light on the truth: Please keep speaking up and speaking out. Please demand integrity within our judiciary, our prosecutors, our law enforcement, our investigative services, and our foster care services.

And to those of you who are still finding the courage to do so, know that your stories matter. They need to be told. It is time to shine light on the darkness and root out the corruption that has allowed this conduct to go on for far too long. Please join me in this call for justice and speak your truth.

#WeToo

—Cynthia L. Clack, J.D.

TABLE OF CONTENTS

FOREWORD

A strange web of coincidences—and fate—led me to a courtroom in Midland, Texas, in 2021, to the child custody trial where I first met Cynthia Clack. A former colleague learned of the case while working with Cynthia on an unrelated matter; it reminded him, he said, of a disturbing case we both covered two decades earlier in Los Angeles family court.

In that case, a mother presented overwhelming evidence that her profoundly disabled daughter—a teenage girl with the mental capacity of a six-year-old—was being sexually abused by her father. Multiple psychologists, doctors, and child welfare professionals supported these allegations. Yet instead of protecting the child, the court turned on the mother. The judge and the father claimed she was "coaching" and "alienating" her daughter. In the end, the distraught woman lost all rights of visitation permanently. It was one of the most inexplicable miscarriages of justice I had ever witnessed, and the memory of it stayed with me through decades of reporting on law, business, and corruption.

My friend urged me to attend the upcoming trial in Midland for a second reason: The young mother Cynthia represented was a family member of a close business associate. This bizarre conjunction of circumstances led me to Midland a few weeks later. As I sat listening to Cynthia's opening statement, I realized with horror that history was repeating itself. Here was another woman desperately trying to protect her children from an abusive father, only to be thwarted by a judge who consistently sided with their abuser. When Cynthia won the trial, I hesitated about whether to take the story any further.

But several details niggled: Witnesses testified under oath to hearing the children describe sex crimes committed against them; why did no criminal investigation follow?

Why did the judge appear to financially punish Cynthia and her client, a stay-at-home mother, by refusing to order the father to pay her outstanding legal fees?

And most disturbingly, why did the judge give the father unsupervised visits with the children, despite overwhelming evidence that he was abusing them and the jury's instruction that their mother receive full custody?

Then Cynthia told me something that made everything snap into focus: She had seen the same patterns, the same accusations, the same outcome for three decades. She had been fighting the same battle over and over on behalf of the children.

That's when I understood that what I was looking at wasn't a series of isolated tragedies; it was a system. She had proof: hundreds of boxes of trial transcripts, depositions, exhibits stored in a warehouse near her Odessa office for decades at a cost of thousands of dollars. I asked why she kept them long after the law required. She said she had been waiting for the day she could reveal everything she had learned.

For the next four years, as I investigated and produced my podcast, *The Devil in Tall City: Child Sex Trafficking in the Bible Belt*, she guided me through a monstrous landscape where a powerful "Club" protected child predators.

I had to unravel this pattern of injustice—clearly not limited to one judge and one jurisdiction—and follow the threads to their evil origins.

Cynthia helped me understand and prove that child sexual abuse and trafficking are not fringe crimes committed by shadowy individuals hiding in the margins of society. They are crimes of power, carried out in plain sight, protected by institutions, enabled by silence. These groups have operated this way since time began, which is precisely why perpetrators so often escape accountability. When people talk about a "deep state," this is the kind of thing they mean: a tacit, unspoken understanding that exposing these crimes would destabilize the very system in which the powerful operate.

It is incredibly dangerous for anyone to challenge or expose these systems; it takes someone of standing, resilience, and high integrity to even attempt it. In Midland, one of the wealthiest communities in America, Cynthia Clack has been pushing against this wall of silence for decades. And she has done it with a persistence and courage that are extraordinary. While law enforcement agencies at the city, state, and federal levels ignored her, she pressed on. While judges overrode juries, she refused to stop. While entire communities looked the other way, Cynthia gathered the evidence, filed the motions, and told the truth.

Her credibility is beyond reproach. Everything she has shown me—reams of court filings, expert testimony, police reports, child welfare assessments—backs up her claims. I have checked for myself, and I do not doubt the veracity of what she presents here. She is, quite simply, a woman who cannot be intimidated out of protecting children.

Cynthia's roots in West Texas run deep. Her great-grandfather served in the Texas House of Representatives in the early 1900s. Her father was a respected district judge in Andrews, Crane, and Winkler Counties. Her stepmother, Barbara Culver Clack, made history as the first woman to serve as a district judge in Midland County before going on to the Texas Supreme Court. The Clack family name carries weight in Midland legal circles. Cynthia could have used that legacy to take an easier path. Instead, she has chosen the hardest one: challenging the very institutions that her family once served, because they have failed to protect the most vulnerable.

That choice comes at great personal cost. Those Midland powers attempted to silence Cynthia with legal and financial threats, as well as crimes against her property. And yet she remains undeterred. In a place where silence is the currency of power, she refuses to be silent. What Cynthia understands—and what this book makes impossible to ignore—is that the abuse of children is not a string of isolated tragedies. It is a system. It is a network of power that survives precisely because it is hidden in plain sight. And until more people find the courage to stand where she stands, it will continue.

I never believed in evil until I saw what I saw in Midland: children betrayed, evidence ignored, abusers protected. But I do believe in courage. And I believe in Cynthia Clack.

She has my immense admiration and respect. She is almost alone on this front, and yet she keeps going. It is my hope that this book will awaken others to what she has been fighting against for so long and that they will join her in the battle to protect children.

—Gina Keating

INTRODUCTION

Almost one in eight of all those in forced labor are children (3.3 million). More than half of these children are in commercial sexual exploitation.[1]

Most likely, anyone reading this book knows what slavery is—essentially a human being owning another human being. We sometimes use the term *slavery* in broader contexts, like when we say that a person is a "slave" to their addiction. Sometimes we describe someone as being a slave to their work. I have even heard people say that a husband treats his wife like a slave or the other way around.

Here in the United States, we say we are a free people, that we are free to live our lives according to our free will and our own personal choices. However, that is not really true. We are limited by many things in an orderly society. For starters, we have laws.

We have laws that say we cannot hit, assault, and injure one another even though we have other laws that say we can own guns and we can legally shoot one another under certain circumstances. We have the right to buy the fanciest, fastest cars we can afford or finance. However, I think it bears mentioning that just because a law says we can have these items, we must still be responsible with them. For example, we can't drive our cars at one hundred miles per hour through a neighborhood or school zone. That would be reckless and irresponsible, would it not?

What if I told you what is happening in some of our cities is equally reckless and irresponsible? Would that upset you? Would it bother you if someone came barreling through your neighborhood at a high speed, with no regard for your safety or the safety and well-being of your family? What if I told you that is exactly what is happening behind closed doors every day in this country? The very people our children, women, and men have been taught they should rely on and trust are the ones who have betrayed them at the deepest possible level.

Our Founding Fathers came to this country to escape the rule of a king in England. They didn't want to be "slaves" to him. They didn't want to be his moneymakers. They didn't want to give the money they were making to King George III and have no say about how it was spent. It incensed them so much they were willing to go to war over it. After winning the war, our courageous Founding Fathers started a new country—a new experiment unlike anything the world had ever seen. It was not perfect then. And it is far from perfect now.

When this country was founded, women did not have the right to vote. They were pretty much the property of their husbands. It wasn't that long ago that wedding vows made women promise to love, honor, and obey (instead of cherish) their spouses. Certainly, there were no divorce lawyers like me to help women be heard in court, much less file for divorce. It took decades upon decades for women to gain the rights and dignity that they have today.

When our early founders moved west, they confronted many obstacles in their drive to take over and "own" the land in this country. The Native Americans fought back. Depending on who is telling the story, they will share their own unique perspective. Were the founders defending their land from entitled men? Or claiming land to start a new life, free from a king?

Were these stories of courage, victory, hardship, or tragedy? It all depends on your perspective. From the viewpoint of the Native Americans who lived on and cared for this land centuries before the Europeans' arrival, our Founding Fathers brought great tragedy and upheaval to their lifestyle and ability to provide for their families.

Many of the early founders of this country owned plantations, and to run and operate these plantations, they owned slaves. It was a way of life. And while it was legal at that time in certain parts of our nation, that fact never made it morally right to own a slave.

The history of human beings capturing, overpowering, and owning other human beings is long and tragic. However, just because it has gone on since the beginning of recorded history does not make it right or acceptable.

A DIFFERENT KIND OF SLAVERY

Today we have a different kind of slavery. It is not legal, and perhaps in some ways, it is more treacherous than any other form. This form of slavery is being practiced and conducted right before our own eyes, yet most people don't recognize it for what it is, much less realize the extent of the calamity.

This form of slavery is what is known as *sex trafficking*. Most people in the United States have heard words and phrases like *human trafficking*, *sexual abuse*, *pedophiles*, *pornography*, *prostitution*, *promotion of prostitution*, and *immigration issues*. Many people have very strong opinions about these words and phrases and are often more than willing to voice their opinions and their solutions. These one-liner solutions are sometimes voiced in reckless catch phrases such as "lock them up," "castrate them," and "give them the death penalty."

Although sex trafficking does involve sexual abuse performed on another human being—and it is often performed by adults on a child—these scenarios are by no means the sole examples of sex trafficking in the United States.

I am writing this book based upon my personal experiences and observations as a board-certified family law specialist by the Texas Board of Legal Specialization. Not many lawyers in Texas have over forty-five years of experience, plus this board certification, because divorce and custody work is a hard, stressful field of practice. Most lawyers who have done this for forty-five years have retired, died, or switched to a different area of law.

My law practice is in the oil-rich part of Texas known as the Permian Basin. It produces oil and gas, which is known as West Texas Crude, setting the benchmark for oil prices in the United States. When I got out of law school in 1978 at the age of twenty-three, I moved to Odessa, Texas, and got a job with a lawyer who had a general law practice.

My early career was exciting, wild, and crazy. We did everything except taxes and intellectual property (patents and copyrights). For those first two and a half years, I was in court regularly, trying everything from traffic tickets and car wrecks to workers' comp and drug cases. We defended a father who sexually molested all four of his daughters and took on personal injury suits pertaining to oil field accidents. We also tried a high-profile murder case and defended a woman who was running prostitution out of her string of massage parlors, who was later charged with attempted murder for shooting her romantic rival in a cheap motel room.

Back in those days, a very well-known story about Odessa was that prostitution and gambling were prolific on a certain floor in an upscale downtown hotel, the Inn of the Golden West. Local law enforcement didn't seem to do much about this business of prostitution. Early in my career, I discovered it was just common knowledge. Everyone knew or had heard about Odessa's "dirty secret." It was like the local crime boss (we all knew, or thought we knew, who that was) had the protection of local law enforcement.

Another thing about Odessa that was pretty well known when I arrived four decades ago was the Oil Show that was put on to showcase and support the petroleum industry. This was a huge event in Odessa, bringing in thousands of people every other year with oil companies, vendors, service companies, and, of course, prostitutes. It was a booming business all the way around. It was the event's reputation and fairly understood that there was a whole lot of alcohol and sex sold in Odessa back then. I wasn't particularly the go-to lawyer for these kinds of cases when people occasionally got arrested, but I did end up with my fair share and had a pretty good glimpse of this modern day Wild West attitude.

Odessa, located in Ector County, Texas, is generally considered the home for oil field workers and service companies that support the oil field. They are the blue-collar workers, whereas the City of Midland, in Midland County, Texas, just to the east, has a totally different reputation. Midland is the city with the more "refined" folks. They, too, have the people who work with the oil industry, but they are generally considered the white-collar, educated geologists, petroleum engineers, and geophysicists. These workers don't get their hands dirty. In fact, they probably don't consider themselves "workers" at all. They are "executives" at worst and "dealmakers" and "owners" at best. They go to work in the tall buildings and dine at the private clubs. They are the people who are creating huge sums of income that turn them into multimillionaires, if they aren't already. Midland is also the home of billionaire Tim Dunn, who is reported by *Texas Monthly* to have powerful influence in both Texas and national politics.[2] In other words, Midland County, Texas, is a place concentrated with people who are politically powerful and financially powerful.

Mailbox money—that is the term frequently used around these parts, and particularly in Midland, to describe the royalty checks, surface damage checks, etc. received as the oil companies do their drilling, strike their black gold, and then pay out the negotiated contracts to the landowners (maybe the heirs of the ranch owners who settled here years ago) or to the savvy dealmakers who put together the drilling of a well that struck the mother lode. This results in mailbox money, and a whole lot of it.

How much? Enough to make Midland County, Texas, the number one wealthiest per capita income county in the state of Texas.[3] Please pause and think about that statistic for a moment. Midland County has the highest per capita income, beating out every other county in the state of Texas. The headlines of the local newspaper, *Midland-Reporter Telegram*, have also bragged that Midland holds second place for that same title for the entire United States. According to the Bureau of Economic Analysis, San Jose–Sunnydale–Santa Clara, California, holds the number one slot.[4]

We are looking at a county with people who receive lots of mailbox money and many who earn lots of money, lots of disposable income. They are well-educated people. There are lots of churches. People say it is a "good" place to raise your children if you have to live in West Texas.

I want you to hold that thought until we get to the end of this book. I have my own opinions, but I'm going to let you be the judge of the goodness of this county as we work our way through each of the chapters together. By the time we get to the end of this book and you have put together some (or all) of the puzzle pieces I have presented and left for you to assemble, you can decide whether what the various clients, witnesses, litigants, and parties are saying is true or if these stories perhaps conceal a darker truth, one that is filled with secrets and events that weave a more sinister tapestry.

Chapter 1

THE CLUB

Ninety-three percent of victims under eighteen knew their abuser; 34 percent were abused by a family member and 59 percent by an acquaintance; only 7 percent were abused by a stranger.[1]

In 1995, I had been practicing law for seventeen years. At this time in my career, I was mainly taking divorce and custody cases. I had just wrapped up a divorce and custody battle that had lasted one and a half years. It had concluded in 1994 with a three-week jury trial in Alpine, Texas, a two-and-a-half-hour drive from Odessa.

My client, the mother, had not won custody. The dad had. When interviewing the jurors afterward, they told me that mainly they had decided to go with the dad because he had the money to employ nannies to get the two young children raised. Both parents had a lot of rough things to say about each other, and they did. The eighteen months leading up to the jury trial had me traveling all over the state of Texas taking the depositions of a multitude of witnesses.

My client had run out of money months before the case was over, but I carried on, doing my best to keep my office going while paying my employees and utilities. Ultimately, the jury awarded $425,000 to my client for her husband's intentional infliction of emotional distress on her. They also awarded me attorney fees of almost half a million dollars. The husband's attorneys made at least $1.8 million on this case. I had seen copies of the canceled checks paid from his trust fund. The husband was an heir to the famous King Ranch family wealth. He didn't work. He was one of the privileged few who collected the mailbox money I spoke of earlier.

A few months after this long, stressful case wrapped up, I settled back into my law practice in Odessa. Soon after, I was hired on a custody case by a client I will refer to as Ele. She was already divorced, and she and her husband had shared custody of their daughter. Both Ele and her ex-husband, whom we'll refer to as Ex, were well educated, each having attained master's degrees. Ele's degree was in counseling, and Ex had a degree in geology. Both of them were highly intelligent. In fact, they were members of MENSA, a group with one requirement: a genius IQ. Ele and Ex had a two-and-a-half-year-old daughter who was a genius too. We'll call the little girl Gee to protect her privacy.

This modification-of-custody lawsuit was filed in Midland by Ex because someone had reported him to Child Protective Services (CPS). The CPS worker began the investigation on Ex and reported some very odd and disturbing conduct by the father. Ex filed this custody suit to get ahead of the CPS report and the fact that Ele would be filing for exclusive custody very soon.

Whoever made the report on Ex had reported that he was French-kissing little Gee goodbye when he dropped her off at day care in the morning. This wasn't a quick peck on the cheek. We're talking long, open-mouth French kissing between a dad and his two-and-a-half-year-old little girl. In addition to that weird, uncomfortable habit, Ex had also made a videotape of little Gee containing a great deal of nudity, including Gee doing various tasks like vacuuming in the nude, as well as lots of bathtub time, bathing in the kitchen sink, etc. The video also had a really odd "random" phone call with Gee on camera carrying on a long conversation with a woman off camera. The woman was calling seemingly to talk with Dad, but Gee answered the phone, and the videotaped conversation just went on and on with this unknown woman.

Little Gee was in her ballerina tutu looking very cute, and her dad's camera was up and rolling when this random phone call came in. Although the camera is running when random woman calls (for Dad, of course), Dad doesn't come right away to take the phone away from Gee to talk to his female friend. He has the video recording Gee and lets Gee go on and on with this conversation. Gee is a brilliant and conversant two-year-old. (She uses words like *copacetic* and *serendipitous* and knows what they mean, according to her mother.) This videotaped conversation did not appear to be scripted on the part of Gee, but it was definitely set up by Dad and the female caller. It certainly depicted Gee as a beautiful, brilliant, and delightful child who could easily carry on an adult conversation with a stranger. At two-and-a-half years old!

Other parts of the video had glimpses of the dad (Ex) appearing in front of the camera while he was filming Gee. Dad was only wearing tighty-whitie underwear when that happened.

Then there was the CPS worker's report from a woman assigned to the case. We will refer to her as Agent 311. Although I didn't know Agent 311 before the case, I knew her husband. She was married to a lawyer whom I had known and been in court with over the years. He had been in the district attorney's office in Odessa and had headed up the prosecution of a murder case when I was one of the defense attorneys representing a young man on a murder charge.

It had been a hard-fought battle in which my client had confessed to a murder he did not commit. My client had been one of several coworkers with a woman who had worked in the janitorial department of the local shopping mall. The murder victim, Velma Nessett, had not shown up for work one morning, and it was discovered later that morning that she had been murdered as she walked from her nearby apartment to the shopping mall.

The murder went unsolved for months. Each time a new detective was assigned to the case, they rounded up the usual suspects and gave each one the third degree. The reason my client, Johnny, was even a blip on their radar was because he had been sent out by his boss to look around in the ditch and inside the culvert on Velma's path as she walked to work just in case she had fallen. Johnny had looked in the culvert. He saw nothing there. Hours later, Velma's body was found in the culvert. Her throat was cut.

The boss commented how Johnny must not have looked at all or didn't look very well. Johnny persisted and insisted that he *did* look. His insistence that he did look and she wasn't there drew attention to him from each detective who picked up this unsolved murder file. The police gave Johnny a lie detector test. They told him that he flunked it, which was actually not true.

During a pretrial hearing, the officer who had told Johnny that he failed the lie detector test when he actually had not testified it was standard operating procedure in the Odessa Police Department to tell someone that they had flunked a lie detector test when that was not the case. This young, simple, poor man had signed a confession to murder while being lied to and bullied by the police. His reasoning was naive. His thought process was that if he signed the confession, the police would quit harassing him. He could then get a trial and "prove" his innocence. He was innocent, but it took many hours of hard work and a long trial to get to the proper outcome. The trial had many fascinating twists and turns, exciting and intriguing. The jury was out for only about forty-five minutes before they came back with a "not guilty" verdict.

The whole time I dealt with Agent 311's husband during this trial, I found him to be honorable and professional. I believe he was as shocked as I was about the police officer's pronouncement that it was "standard operating procedure" to lie to a suspect about flunking a lie detector test.

Now I was working on a case with the assistant prosecutor's wife. She seemed to be honorable and professional as well. Agent 311 was a seasoned CPS worker and was on the job right away, investigating Ele's ex-husband, the father of Gee. She went to Ex's apartment. She looked around and in her report described that Ex had several books in his bookshelves on satanic ritualistic abuse. One book was titled *Lucifer's Handbook*. Her initial report stated she believed Ex was involved in these practices because of things her initial investigation revealed. She made recommendations that Gee should not be left in Dad's care and possession unsupervised.

This was the first time in my career to see a CPS report calling out satanic ritualistic abuse. I suppose I had a concept in my mind that such things existed, but really, I thought it was only subject matter for Hollywood screenwriters who wrote scripts for horror movies. This report was talking about a well-educated man, a genius geologist, who was into not only worshipping the Devil but also practicing ritualistic abuse. Dad's activities had gone so far as to raise numerous red flags to the person who called in the report to Child Protective Services, but they had also caught the total attention of a seasoned CPS worker who made this initial investigation and wrote this report.

As novel and strange as these facts were to me, the next things that happened in the case were even more shocking. District Judge Dean Rucker, in the 318th Judicial Court of Midland, where the case was being heard, wrote a scathing letter attacking Agent 311!

Let's pause for a moment. Here I am, newly hired by a mom on a child custody case, which is my board-certified specialty. And while the facts are very strange, I felt I was totally equipped, both professionally and maturely, to handle this case. I had previously worked on a criminal case dealing with an incestuous pedophile father who sexually molested all of his daughters. I had also tried some murder cases. Naively, I thought I was tough and pretty worldly since I had all this experience and had seen *The Exorcist* back in the 1970s.

On top of all of my personal experience, I was surrounded by a family full of lawyers. My daddy was a lawyer and had been the district judge of the 109th District Court for Andrews, Winkler, and Crane Counties during the 1980s. My older brother was a lawyer and had been county attorney for years in Crane, Texas. My younger brother was a top-notch lawyer in the fields of personal injury law and civil trial. He also held the record for highest monetary jury verdicts in personal injury cases in more than one county in Texas. My stepmother had been the county judge in Midland, then the district judge of the 318th Judicial District Court in Midland, and later served as a justice on the Texas Supreme Court before she retired. In other words, among my family members' careers and mine, we possessed quite a variety and range of legal experiences and situations involving litigation.

When my stepmother, Barbara Culver Clack, received her appointment to the Supreme Court in the late 1980s, the judge who replaced her in the 318th Judicial District Court in Midland was Dean Rucker. By 1995, Dean Rucker had a few years' experience on the bench, hearing and ruling on divorces and custody disputes in Midland. He had the reputation around the state for being smart and knowledgeable in the field of family law. He was, and continues to be, a frequent speaker at family law seminars and continuing education. According to his current resume posted on the Midland County website, he has received a multitude of awards over the years, including being the 2014 recipient of the Samuel Pessarra Outstanding Jurist Award given by the Texas Bar Foundation. In 2006, he was awarded the Chair's Award of Excellence by the Texas Center for the Judiciary. Judge Rucker was also honored as the 2005 Jurist of the Year by the Texas Chapter of the American Academy of Matrimonial Lawyers. In 1997, Texas CASA (Court Appointed Special Advocates) recognized Judge Rucker as the Clayton E. Evans Judge of the Year. He was a charter commissioner on the Supreme Court of Texas Permanent Judicial Commission for Children, Youth, and Families and now acts as one of its jurists in residence. Judge Rucker is also the past chair of the Texas Children's Justice Act Task Force.[2] Based upon his plaques, trophies, and awards, he is certainly one of the most honored and recognized judges in the state of Texas in the field of family law.

Let's go back to the year 1995 and Judge Rucker's scathing letter attacking Agent 311 regarding what she had to say about Ex, his conduct regarding Gee, and his satanic ritualist books on his bookshelves in his apartment.

Judge Dean Rucker wrote the following:

Mrs. (Ele) raises concerns for the safety of the child and accuses Mr. (Ex) of sexually inappropriate conduct with the child.

Specifically, she accuses Mr. (Ex) of fondling the child vaginally; sleeping with the child when the child is not wearing panties; stroking the child's chest and buttocks; kissing the child in a prolonged, open-mouthed manner; forcing the child to place her buttocks over his genital area; and videotaping the child for extended periods while she is either nude or in her panties.

The Court admitted into evidence a videotape made by Mr. (Ex). Agent 311 suggests that the videotape shows that the child was nude for several hours at a time and finds fault with Mr. (Ex)'s manner of videotaping. Specifically, Agent 311 objects to a segment of the videotape in which Mr. (Ex) filmed the child walking up some steps and coming down the same. In it, the child is filmed from behind, and she bends over to support herself as she is going down the steps, her skirt hikes up, exposing her underwear. Although the action depicted in the videotape is nothing more than a three-year-old child having some difficulty coming down the steps in rubber boots, Agent 311 attaches a sexual connotation to this segment.

In another segment, Mr. (Ex) acquiesces to the child's request to look through the camera and he and the child are standing in front of a mirror. As Mr. (Ex) places the camera in front of the child, he places his hand on her left shoulder. Agent 311 found this to be "interesting" and notes that when Mr. (Ex) removed his hand from the child's shoulder, he seemed to place it on his "crotch."

Agent 311's conclusions about these segments are indicative of her lack of objectivity and her overreaction to two very innocuous events. In the segment in which Mr. (Ex) places his hand on the child's shoulder, it is patently obvious he is steadying the child while he holds the camera to her face. There is absolutely nothing sexually suggestive or inappropriate about his touching her. How Agent 311 concludes that he placed his hand on his "crotch" when he removed it from the child's shoulder defies credibility since it is impossible to see what Mr. (Ex) did with his hand when he removed it from the child's shoulder.

There is no need to go through other events depicted on the videotape. While there are moments of nudity by the child depicted on the videotape, these are quite brief and harmless. The videotape is nothing more than a celluloid scrapbook of a child who displays no fear of her father. There is no suggestion of pedophilia or sexual abuse. Agent 311's conclusions about the videotape seriously compromise the credibility of the remainder of her testimony.

Very truly yours,
Dean Rucker

This letter was written by the district judge after hearing the first temporary hearing, and it had the predictable effect intended by the judge. It got Agent 311 removed from working on this case any further since the judge had stated that her conclusions seriously compromised the credibility of the remainder of her testimony. Other CPS workers were assigned to the case to investigate and monitor Ex and his conduct with his daughter.

I was shocked by the fierceness of the contents of this letter. The fact that the judge was maligning the CPS worker assigned to the case was very unusual to me. It also seemed very unusual for the judge to write a letter attacking her.

When a modification of custody case is filed in Texas, the petitioner (here it was Ex) files an Original Petition to Modify the existing order (the divorce decree). The respondent (mom, Ele) files an answer and perhaps a counterpetition setting forth her requested change to the divorce decree. One or both lawyers request a temporary hearing. This hearing is usually set and conducted within three to fourteen days of the time the responding party is served.

Things can happen very quickly at this point. Witnesses are served with subpoenas to appear for the temporary hearing. The parties, their lawyers, and the witnesses show up, testify, and give evidence to the judge and state their requested relief. The judge hears all of this and makes an initial ruling, usually at the end of the hearing, from the bench. Sometimes, if the judge has to review extensive records, the judge will take the case under advisement and send a letter to the lawyers telling us what the ruling is, and then one of the lawyers prepares a temporary order incorporating the judge's ruling.

Typically, this temporary order remains in place until the final trial. Sometimes one or both lawyers request to come back to court through motions to modify the temporary orders to request a change or clarification. The final trial is when each side brings forth all their evidence, seeking their ultimate relief. Most times, that final hearing or trial is many months down the road, after depositions and discovery are conducted, but the first hearing is typically set and heard very quickly. Usually, I have only known my client for a few days when

I am going in to argue and present their case to the judge at the temporary hearing.

The lawyers have the responsibility to cross-examine and punch holes in the credibility of the witness's testimony. In this case, it was up to Ex's lawyer to cross-examine and question Agent 311 as to what she saw in Dad's apartment. It was Ex's lawyer's job to question the workers at the child's day care who saw Dad giving the long French kisses to his daughter.

The thing that was so strange and out of the ordinary about Judge Rucker's letter was that his ruling or findings after the first hearing with testimony and cross-examination, including other evidence in the courtroom, was an intense attack against the CPS worker, Agent 311, and how the judge's remarks strongly discounted her investigation and conclusions. For me, the shock wasn't just in what the father had done but in how swiftly the system turned its fire on the very investigator who tried to sound the alarm.

PUZZLE PIECES

Following are some puzzles pieces I have laid out for you in this chapter in the way of questions. Please keep them in mind as you read on to see whether they are part of a larger puzzle or merely isolated incidents.

- Why did the father video multiple scenarios of the child while she was nude, vacuuming around the house, and bathing?
- Why do you think Ex recorded his daughter carrying on a long conversation with a woman she didn't even know over the phone instead of taking the call himself?

- Why did the father edit the video to showcase the daughter's comfort and ability to talk to a stranger?
- Why did the father film the daughter while he was in his underwear, and why did he choose to reveal himself in his underwear in the edited version?
- Why did the judge not discuss or seem concerned about a father French-kissing his daughter in front of day care workers?
- Why was the judge not concerned about the father doing his filming of the daughter while he was in his underwear?
- Why did the judge not demonstrate any questions or concerns for the safety of the child when the seasoned CPS worker had testified regarding her observations, including the satanic ritualist books in the father's apartment?
- Why would a highly respected district judge, with accolades in the field of family law and child protection, reprimand a CPS worker for recommending supervised visitation after discovering disturbing content and behavior in Ex's home on one of her visits?
- Are there similar situations in your community? If so, how do you think those in authority affect the safety of the child?

Chapter 2

FEAR AND MIND CONTROL

"Coercive control is a calculated strategy of domination. A perpetrator begins by grooming their victim, thereby gaining trust and access. They then make their victim afraid—usually, but not always, by instigating the fear of physical or sexual violence. Fear is what makes threats credible. And it is when a threat is credible that a demand becomes coercive."[1]

As I worked on this case for Ele, the facts that were unfolding were increasingly disturbing. The child was reporting all kinds of "games" she and Daddy had played. One was called Tangle-Tangle, where Daddy tied her up while she was naked and then he licked her all over her body. Gee described that Daddy loaded bullets into his gun and then inserted the gun into her vagina. Yes, Gee knew all the correct names for her body parts. She didn't name the gun as a revolver, but that's what she was describing to the caseworker, based on Gee's details of how he loaded the bullets. In front of one of the CPS workers, Gee asked her daddy if he was going to show the workers his gun.

The facts of this case were getting stranger and more twisted by the day. I needed to have a better understanding of what I was really dealing with, so I decided to find a consultant or an expert—not necessarily to testify but one who could explain some things to me.

Interestingly and fortunately, I had met a woman about three years earlier at a meeting attended by a group of therapists and counselors to help them recognize issues arising out of ritualistic cult abuse. The woman speaking at this gathering had grown up in a family who were members of the satanic cult. According to what she told the group of counselors (and me), everyone in her family was in "the cult." This included her grandparents, aunts, uncles, cousins—everybody. Her mother had left and broken off from the cult, and so had she. The woman described how hard it had been to leave the cult. They had been stalked, threatened, and tormented—you name it. The people tormenting her mother had even placed an upside-down cross in their yard and burned it. She further described what it was like growing up in the cult. She said that it made such a lasting impression on her because they controlled their members through fear and mind control.

BRAINWASHING

This former cult member explained that the leaders kept people in line through intimidation and also by lying to them and telling them how to think. I don't recall her using the phrase *brainwashing*, but that was my impression of what the cult leaders were doing. If anyone questioned or challenged their lies or beliefs, the person who questioned anything was brought back in line through fear and intimidation tactics or by outright lying to the person to get them to question what they had just witnessed.

Gaslighting is a term that has become commonly used in our society these days. I interpret it to mean a tactic used by an individual to cause another person to question and doubt the truthfulness of what they have just experienced. The gaslighter bullies the other person into questioning the truth. When multiple people in the cult used tactics of intimidation and lies, it could cause the victim to question their own reality or version of events more strongly. Gaslighting is certainly a tactic employed by the cult, and not just the satanic cult. This kind of bullying and brainwashing is being used by multiple people and groups in our society to cause others to doubt what their own experiences reveal.

She described the threats and terrorist tactics imposed upon her and other children of the cult while she was growing up. Her sister had witnessed someone strap a bomb onto a child and then the child was murdered, blown up right before the eyes of onlooking children. They were told if they challenged or questioned anything, this, too, would be their fate, or maybe it would be done to their brother, sister, or their parents.

This meeting with the woman in the early 1990s had made quite an impression on me. I reached out to my counselor friend who had originally introduced me to the former cult member. I wanted to explore the possibility of her consulting with me on Ele's case. She agreed to travel to Odessa, look at the evidence, and tell me whether she thought, based on her own experience, I was dealing with a case involving the satanic cult.

For many hours, she studied the evidence and shared her opinions and observations about what I was dealing with. She said the satanic cult is, among other things, basically organized crime. In addition to the parts about their rituals and robes, they are into prostitution and pornography involving both adults and children. She said the cult was making vast amounts of money through both child and adult pornography and prostitution. She said it was her opinion that the video Ex had put together was actually an "audition" video to showcase Gee for child pornography and prostitution. A child this beautiful and brilliant would bring a lot of money to this horrifying world where children are used, bought, and sold.

The consultant explained that the cult had many people from every walk of life and in very high and powerful places. She stated they had their "tentacles" everywhere. Obviously, in most places, members of the cult didn't announce or publicly acknowledge their membership. They didn't have a satanic church in every town, where the members openly went to practice their "freedom of religion." San Francisco, California, is the only place I have heard of where they openly have a satanic church.

Years ago, I had a friend who confided in me that he had joined the Church of Satan in San Francisco. At the time my friend told me about his membership, I didn't know any of these things that this consultant was telling me. My friend had been a funny and delightful man, with no signs of ongoing criminal participation or ritualist abuse. I really didn't put much thought or energy into what my friend had told me. In my mind, he had joined the Church of Satan and given his soul to the Devil because he was gay, and this was his statement of defiance against the Christians who had said he was damned to hell for his sexuality and lifestyle. He didn't seem like a bad or evil person, so I just didn't think much about it.

The consultant went on to explain that the cult members had to have a place to gather to perform their rituals and conduct their meetings. Since this was all very much secret and generally taboo in our society, the cult members met in a variety of places, sometimes even in Christian churches. "It's just secretive," she said. She added it might be in the basement of a Christian church where they would actually carry out their rituals. She said it could be any organization where the cult members gathered to do their rituals, but no one outside of the cult would know or suspect anything out of order.

When they gathered, these members needed a cover for what they were really doing. The organization serving as the cover could be anything: church, Boy Scouts, garden club, social club, and so on. She said the members were generally not suspected of anything out of the ordinary, and the people in their community thought they were great citizens: "Oh, he's a great guy, always at church" or "always working with the Boy Scouts."

Perhaps these things she described to me are the reason it is so hard for us to believe that something so sinister is going on with people who appear to be so nice, so pleasant, so good with children, so active in good organizations. It is also why children are not being listened to and acknowledged when they report abuse by an adult. We just don't want to believe that someone who appears to be good is such a monster as to abuse a child. It is even harder to believe that there is a group of people gathered together who are worshipping the Devil, abusing children, using them, and offering them up to the world for pornography and prostitution. But this woman, who had grown up in a family that had practiced satanic worship and rituals for generations, was telling me how powerful and pervasive the entire network was. She said they had their well-placed people in all aspects of society, including in the government, positions as judges, workers in law enforcement, investigative agencies, and journalism.

She said by having their well-placed people in every area, the cult could help other cult members when abuse was reported or criminal charges were filed. Someone in the cult could catch and stop the initial complaint, or someone higher up in the organization could quash the investigation as it progressed if it wasn't stopped early on.

This vast network of well-placed cult members was what I came to understand as the organized-crime aspect of the cult. This part was not necessarily ritualistic worship. Instead, it carried on and protected the activities of abuse perpetuated by other cult members, such as child pornography, child prostitution, and sex trafficking. These well-placed cult members not only protected the predators and abusers who were a part of their cult; they also protected those who supported them, as they all belonged to the same "Club." It was as though they had a playbook where they instructed members to attack and threaten the righteous people who reported the abuse, the sex trafficking, and other crimes. These Club members used tactics of fear and intimidation on those who dared to report their activities or tried to stop them.

In 1995, I learned many things from this consultant who had grown up in a family vastly different from my own. Although my consultant and I were close to the same age, she had grown up with relatives who worshipped the Devil. It was somewhat hard for me to imagine there were actually families, extended families, and generations of families who did that. I had grown up in a family where my mother made sure we were in regular attendance at the First Baptist Church. We attended Sunday school, the Sunday morning church service, Training Union on Sunday night (a kind of Sunday school at night for Baptists), and the Wednesday night church service. I was an active participant with Girls Auxiliary, where I learned

Bible verses and progressed through annual ceremonies recognizing my accomplishments with this group. I was a very good Southern Baptist girl. Through the advancement of Girls Auxiliary, I earned a crown, a cape, and a scepter to signify my progress, discipline, and participation in memorizing Bible scriptures and doing various projects that reflected Christian principles and teachings.

Although the sermons I heard from the pulpit talked about the Devil and Satan and the evils of such a being, my understanding was much along the lines that Jesus had dealt with him two thousand years ago, and all of that was done and in the past. The "sinful" things I heard about were the evils of drinking (alcoholic beverages such as whiskey and beer) and the evils of dancing. We had a whole lot of guilt imposed on us as children and teenagers about going to dances, including the prom. Dancing was evil because it led to sex. My concept and trust in these Baptist rules and dogma came to a shattering halt when I attended the wedding of one of my best friends, who was also very entrenched in Southern Baptist teachings. Her daddy was a deacon at the First Baptist Church. In fact, there were several deacons from our church at that wedding reception. All of them were dancing, and they were the best dancers on the dance floor. Their hypocrisy was not lost on me.

Even though I was coming to my own understanding, opinions, and beliefs regarding the dogma and spiritual matters, the shattering of denominational rules and observations of contradictions, inconsistencies, and hypocrisy never shook my belief in God, Jesus, and the Holy Spirit. It just knocked down the pedestals I had placed people on and made me question and let go of the dogma and rules that no longer made sense to me. Throughout my life, I have questioned, read, studied, and pondered, always seeking the truth. I have a logical mind. I was trained as a debater and to use critical thinking. This training and practice are important, and they have served me well.

Beyond logical thinking, training, and education, I believe we have within us a core essence that knows the truth and seeks the truth. I call it our inner voice. Many people over the ages have written about this inner voice through books and songs. I believe this inner voice is what speaks to us and speaks the truth. Many people have trouble hearing it because they are too busy. They don't turn down the noise. These days, many people are too busy looking at their electronic devices or social media threads. Our inner voices are trying to speak to us, but the lies and dogma are demanding our time and attention. Until we get still and listen to our inner voice, we will be controlled and misled by someone with an agenda to own, control, or manipulate us.

I never asked my consultant how it was that she and her mother had broken off from the satanic cult, nor did I ask where she currently was in her spiritual beliefs and practices. This was a woman who had experienced a family and childhood so vastly different from mine that I was still trying to comprehend her explanation of the cult. My inner voice told me to stay focused, to listen to and learn from her.

What I was told by this consultant was that this cult was vast, it extended into all aspects of our society, and it was *secret*. Up until this point, my idea of a cult was that it consisted of a small group of misguided, brainwashed people who followed a crazy or evil leader like Charles Manson or Jim Jones. These cult leaders got their followers to commit murder or "drink the Kool-Aid." I had read the book *Helter Skelter* by Curt Gentry and Vincent Bugliosi, the prosecutor in the trial of the murders committed by Manson's followers. And I had read articles about the tragic ending in Jonestown, where the followers of Jim Jones (willingly and some not so willingly) drank the poisonous concoction resulting in an act of mass suicide.

My limited awareness of cults was not adequate enough to encompass what this consultant was telling me about the satanic cult. She was born into a family that had been worshipping the Devil for generations. Somehow, she and her mother woke up and decided to get out. Yet there are others who voluntarily and intentionally join the satanic cult. Others are drawn into it through naivety, ignorance, or neglect. By the end of my time with the consultant, I was convinced I had an idea of what I was dealing with regarding the custody battle of Gee.

Now I was left with a big question: What was I going to do about it? I needed to represent my client to the best of my ability, and we had her daughter to protect. I knew I had my work cut out for me and that Judge Rucker was not giving any credence or concern to the report of Agent 311 regarding the dad's disturbing conduct or his satanic books. Not one to be deterred, I paid a jury fee and requested a jury trial. From that point on, I decided to call this group The Club, because it seemed to me that its reaches extended far beyond its inner circle of worship.

PUZZLE PIECES

In this chapter, I have some additional puzzle pieces for you to assemble by way of questions. As with the first chapter, keep these pieces in mind as you work your way through this book.

- Do you find it disturbing that a father created "games" involving bondage, nudity, and guns with his two-year-old?

- Have you ever observed the practices of fear, intimidation, and gaslighting to keep victims and families silent?
- Do you think Ex's videotape of Gee was an "audition" video for pornography and prostitution, or was it more innocent, like the judge suggested?
- What happens when people in positions of power belong to or are controlled by a network of protection of predators?
- Have you ever observed or seen evidence of organizations or groups in your own community being used as covers for abuse?
- Is it significant to normalize the child being videotaped while she is nude?

Chapter 3

PAYING ATTENTION

Recantation is common after disclosure (and often linked to family pressure). About 23 percent of substantiated child sexual-abuse disclosures were later recanted in a large well-cited case-file study—with recantation linked to a child's dependency on family and pressure from adults.[1]

The summer of 1995 was full of spiritual lessons for me. I had become accustomed to odd and strange things happening around me at my office, my home, and even when I was away from home. For some reason, these strange events always seemed to involve electronics. Over the years, I have experienced a television coming on by itself. And when the TV came on, there would be an angel on the screen. Other times, the radio would start playing without my turning it on or even being nearby, and the song would have comforting lyrics, like they were a message from God. Another time, a broken answering machine, which had been unplugged for weeks, was suddenly working again (and plugged in). The message left by the caller was regarding a seminar on miracles I was considering attending—*a seminar on miracles!* It seemed that these messages from the spiritual world were happening with increasing frequency. Maybe they had always been happening and I had just been ignoring or discounting them. Eventually, when I started putting my own puzzle pieces together about these events, I could not think of any other logical or reasonable explanation, so I just called it a God thing. And whenever things like this happened, I decided to stop and pay attention to the message and quit being freaked out over how it happened to come to me.

It wasn't just the God things with the electronics that were coming to my awareness that summer of 1995. I was also beginning to have a greater consciousness of spiritual matters. I started paying attention to things in a way that I never had previously.

I suppose I have always believed in angels. They are an important part of the Bible stories of my childhood. Of course, as a good Southern Baptist girl, I had that unquestioning belief that there were spiritual beings around sometimes, specifically aware of us mortals. For the most part, though, I didn't particularly believe they interacted with us. I thought they had more important things to do, like playing the harp or singing in the Heavenly Choir. I didn't really believe that I had one or more angels who actively cared and watched over my daily life. After all, much of my time was spent reading divorce decrees, preparing interrogatories, taking depositions, and consulting and counseling with clients. Why would these high-powered spiritual beings be hanging around me?

Yet I had read quite a few books about angels and their interactions with humans. I loved the stories about how people saw a being of light and something miraculous happened. Maybe it was a healing. Maybe it was a message. Maybe it was a miracle. I loved the thought that we had angels around us. I just didn't believe I had ever seen one or experienced the presence of one in my life. To me, angels represented the good things in the spiritual world. They were gifts from God. In the same way, I believed the stories in the Bible that there are fallen angels who rebelled against God.

I certainly was no expert on the fallen angels. Names like the Devil, Lucifer, Satan, and Caligastia kind of fit into that category of those bad, rebellious spiritual beings. In the year 2000, I learned about and read a book called *The Urantia Book,* which was fascinating and truly one of the best books I've ever read. It is about two thousand pages long, so it took me a while to read it. That book gave a good description of Lucifer and the Lucifer Rebellion. It tells who Satan and Caligastia are and the role they played in this universal spiritual war. It also sets out the Lucifer manifesto. This book gave me a better understanding of the stories and teachings I had heard in my childhood spiritual lessons. I found the book to be fascinating, intriguing, and thought provoking, but I didn't have the benefit of reading it until five years after my meetings with the consultant in Ele's case.

As I worked with Ele on her custody case, the strange and bizarre facts continued to unfold. I took the deposition of experts and fact witnesses. I read reports from CPS workers and supervisors. The CPS workers continued to report disturbing things about Ex's activities and conduct regarding Gee. For example, he was obsessed with the desire to nurse her, and he wanted to seek medical intervention so he could produce milk and suckle her at his breast. Upon hearing these stories, we requested another temporary hearing, and by this time, the evidence was so disturbing and unusual that Judge Rucker ordered that all of Ex's visitation with Gee be supervised by CPS workers.

Ex would show up at the supervised visitation with a great big picture book in which each picture depicted a busy scene with multiple characters doing a multitude of activities. At first glance, it might appear that the scenes were of a happy and innocent day at the beach or a circus. However, more careful observation of the drawings of the characters revealed that some of the pages showed a person with a knife pointed at a child with a drop of blood coming off the blade. Another page depicted a child urinating, another showed a child being choked by someone, and so on.

When Ex showed up for his visits with the giant book, he would speak German to Gee as he pointed at various pictures. Initially, the CPS supervisor thought this was great; Daddy was teaching his genius daughter German during his visitation periods. Of course, the supervisor didn't understand German, so she didn't really know what Ex was saying to Gee. It just looked sweet and caring that this daddy was teaching his daughter a foreign language.

I asked my consultant about the giant picture book, which was maybe twenty-four inches tall and eighteen inches wide, and she told me it was similar to something she had seen used by the cult in her childhood. She said it was a way to communicate threats or discretely share instructions by pointing to the pictures. She said it was very likely that Ex was doing exactly that to Gee right under the nose of the CPS supervisor. Upon learning this, we requested an order from the court that all communication be done in English during the supervised visits and that the picture book not be brought back to visitations.

During the course of this investigation, the inappropriate activities with Gee were not the only scenarios with a child involved. There was testimony in the jury trial that a group of men who were friends of Ex would participate in a sweat lodge together. They called themselves The Clan of the Frogmen. It was explained that there was a ceremonial event in which the adult men were all naked in an enclosed room or tent where they had a fire or hot coals to bring them to an intense sweat. It was supposed to be a spiritually enlightening experience in the nature of an Indigenous ceremony. The concern I had from this testimony was that they had one boy about twelve years old who was naked and participating in the sweat lodge with them. When this fact came out in open court, with Judge Rucker on the bench and a full courtroom of observers, I looked around the courtroom to see whether anyone looked shocked or disturbed about testimony regarding several naked men exposing themselves and sweating with a boy in their midst.

However, there was no reaction or comment about this event by the judge. I was continually asking myself more questions like, *Why was Dean Rucker angry about CPS worker Agent 311 reporting about satanic ritualist abuse, yet he does not even comment about the sworn testimony of these adult men exposing themselves to a preteen boy while they are going through a ritualistic ceremony of sweating, trying to get high?* This apparent lack of concern on the part of the judge was obvious and concerning to me.

PUZZLE PIECES

The following puzzle pieces are meant to press deeper into the unsettling details—challenging you to question how behaviors, symbols, and courtroom reactions expose hidden dangers around children.

- Why do you think children recant abuse disclosures?
- Why would a father express a desire to medically induce lactation and nurse his toddler?

- What does it suggest when a parent at a supervised visitation brings a large picture book whose images include violence and sexualized scenes?
- Why would a parent use a foreign language during supervised visits to communicate with the child through pictures?
- How might a picture book be used as a covert method to signal threats or instructions to a child?
- What does testimony about a preteen boy participating naked in adult sweat lodge ceremonies reveal about the circle of associates around Ex?
- Why would a judge respond strongly to an investigator's report about alleged ritual abuse yet show little reaction to sworn testimony about adults and a naked child in a ceremonial setting?

Chapter 4

A VERDICT

In cases in which a mother alleges child sexual abuse, the court "credits" (finds credible) that claim only 15 percent of the time.[1]

As I worked on the case, preparing for the jury trial, I had to make a decision about how I was going to handle this issue involving the cult. The whole cast of characters and the testimony surrounding this case were full of odd and strangely twisted people and facts.

Ultimately, I made the decision not to mention anything about the satanic cult in front of the jury. Instead, I would present facts about this very inappropriate conduct by this dad and his very strange and inappropriate band of friends and associates. They may have been geniuses, but their conduct was such that I believed twelve West Texas jurors from Midland would get the point without my trying to label them as satanic cult worshippers.

On top of the many bizarre facts, there was a murder and a death ruled as a suicide in the circle of Ex's disturbing world. One month before this trial began, Gee's grandfather murdered her grandmother! Right before trial, Ex took Gee to a state up north to attend her grandmother's funeral while her granddad was locked up in jail for the murder.

As though the fact of this family murder wasn't weird enough, a few months earlier, Ex had been traveling with Gee by train from Chicago to the city where the grandparents had lived. On a train ride of less than two hours, Ex and Gee met a random woman who became so captivated by observing the great relationship between Ex and Gee that she later attended the funeral of Ex's mother after she was murdered. At the jury trial, this same random woman came to testify as a character witness for Ex and to tell the jury what a great daddy he was on that train ride and about their "coincidental" meeting months earlier.

I questioned this woman on the witness stand regarding how odd it was for her to attend the funeral of a woman she didn't know, combined with the fact that she had only met Ex, the murdered woman's son, a few months earlier and spoken with him for less than two hours. Her reply was along the lines of "Oh no, after all, I attend over four hundred funerals a year." This response was, to this day, perhaps one of the most unusual answers to my cross-examination of a witness in all of my forty-eight years of practicing law.

Another death occurred among the friends of the MENSA group around this time. The story of his demise was that this man committed suicide, but I was told there was no evidence of depression. Also of note, there wasn't really any evidence that the authorities even conducted an investigation on his death.

MIND GAMES

Besides the disturbing facts and evidence surrounding children, the murder, and suspicious "suicide" of the MENSA member, there were also events I will describe as mind games. While the case was pending, Ele had to vacate her home for a few weeks and live in a motel because her residence needed some repairs. One day, she came back to the motel room after work, and her room key did not work. She went to the front desk to inquire about it, and the person helping her treated Ele like she had lost her mind. She was told, "Of course that is not your room. Here is your proper room key." Confused, Ele took her new room key and went to the new room. When she walked into this new room, all of her belongings were in there in the exact arrangement and location as they had been in her prior room, just as she had left them that morning—even down to the used Kleenex she had left on the nightstand.

This incident was a clear message to Ele (and to me) that The Club could and would get to you anytime they wanted. For the motel employee to act like Ele had requested the room change and she was the one who was crazy or suffering from some mental lapse was an example of gaslighting in overdrive. However, this mind game went far beyond some of the tactics I have seen spouses pull on one another during divorces and domestic squabbles.

This event of moving all of Ele's contents from one room to another took the help and coordination of motel employees. To Ele's knowledge, there was no one in Ex's circle of friends and associates who worked at a motel. His group consisted of geniuses with advanced degrees, not housekeepers and clerks at a motel.

When Ele informed me about the motel room exchange and how the employees acted as though she were crazy or confused, I went back to the things that my consultant had told me about The Club. They had well-placed people everywhere. Whether the people who moved her belongings in her room were a part of The Club or whether they were simply paid off we never knew. What is certain is they were messing with Ele, playing a mental game. But I had to wonder, what was their end game? To make her more anxious? Did they bug her room? And what, if anything, was coming next?

There were other examples of tricks and stunts pulled during the year I was working on Ele's case. One day, the doorbell rang at my home. When I answered the door, no one was there, but there was a pile of torn-up pieces of paper on my doorstep. I noticed there was something written on the pieces of paper, but it wasn't English. The symbols were written in green ink, and they looked like archaic lettering, something like ancient runes. I never knew what it was, and I didn't follow up on any kind of investigation. This was just another mind game they were playing.

Was it supposed to be a spell or a hex? I didn't know. As far as I was concerned, it was some rude person who had left their litter on my doorstep. My life was going on, but I definitely believed this little pile of confetti was related to some of the antics of the band of characters in what I was now calling The Club.

As the summer of 1995 passed and I moved through the developments of Ele's custody case, I was learning many lessons and an entirely new way to view the world around me. I had never realized there was such an organized and united group of people whose goals and activities were directed toward abuse and evil. Of course, I was aware of the existence of such entities: organized crime syndicates, gangs, cartels, and the like. I knew there were people who joined together to steal or cheat to line their pockets with money. I knew there were people whose love of money and/or power was so great they would willingly break the laws of our nation and state. I also knew there were plenty of weak and fearful people who were willing to turn their heads and not acknowledge the abuse and abusers. Unfortunately, those people whose job it was to enforce and uphold the laws of our state and nation many times found it easier, or perhaps more lucrative, to ignore the violations, particularly if they were conducted by someone rich or powerful.

SEX TRAFFICKING

Regarding crimes involving sex trafficking, I saw news stories of the prosecution of women who were on the streets soliciting men to pay them for sex. These women were usually busted by undercover cops in a sting operation. I saw the results of raids on the "dirty bookstores" and establishments that sold pornographic movies, books, magazines, and paraphernalia. This usually happened right before local elections so the county attorney could say they were tough on crime and active in cleaning up these sordid activities in our community. Odessa had a reputation for having hookers and porn shops. There was the constant ebb and flow of rounding up and shutting down these immoral businesses. Eventually, the women on the street would reappear, and the shops would open again under new ownership or management.

Since I no longer represented people in criminal cases by the year 1995, I really wasn't in court to observe the prosecution and defense of crimes regarding the pornography and prostitution cases in Odessa. The people in Midland County, just to the east of Odessa, liked to point out that they were different. They didn't seem to have the problem of the seedy sex trafficking and prostitution that Odessa, in Ector County, had. Midland didn't have the stores that sold the X-rated movies and books. It seemed the people in Midland prided themselves on being a community that was wholesome and moral, while arrogantly pointing their fingers at Odessa for being so sinful.

I lived in Odessa because it was the town where I moved in 1978 after law school. I was married when I graduated from law school, and my husband was offered a job in Odessa. His job was with the Shafer Law Firm. This firm was full of prominent, accomplished lawyers. We were happy for him to work there and thought it would be no problem for me to get a job.

As it turned out, getting a job offer for me wasn't as easy as I thought. I went through approximately fifty interviews before I was hired by a lawyer who gave me a job paying $1,000 per month. It puzzled me that no one (until the fiftieth interview) wanted to hire me. I was the third female lawyer in town. Looking back, I realize there was a whole lot of doubt on the part of the male lawyers that a woman could or would be an asset to their office or firm. I was determined that I would not only be the best woman lawyer in my field but the best lawyer.

Being a female in those days may have been a barrier in being considered to be hired for a job, but it turned out to be an advantage once I actually went to work and got into the courtroom. The judges and other lawyers really paid attention to the novelty of having a woman come into the courtroom and really do a great job. Once they realized I was prepared, I was a fighter, and I could win cases, my reputation among the lawyers and judges began to grow. It also expanded throughout the community, and I began to get hired on a variety of cases.

After two and a half years of working for the man who gave me my first job, I left to open my own office as a sole practitioner. I stayed in Odessa, keeping both my home and my office in Odessa. As I became more specialized in the area of family law, my reputation grew to the extent that clients from counties two hundred miles or more away would travel to Odessa to hire me for their divorces and custody battles. I wasn't advertising, so these people were hiring me by word-of-mouth reputation and the referrals of former clients and other lawyers.

The fact that I was being hired to represent people in many different counties in Texas allowed me the opportunity to try cases in front of many different judges. This wide variety of experience in a broad range of courtrooms presided over by judges with individual styles gave me a very good measure of how judges conduct themselves. Of course, I didn't always agree with the way a judge ruled in a case. I vetted my cases and clients carefully and chose to represent people I thought I could and wanted to help, so my desire to work on their cases increased and gave me the passion to work diligently for them. By this point in my career, I rarely ended up with clients I didn't like, I didn't believe in, or whose cases I harbored doubts about.

Ele's case—the facts, witnesses, and events—were so different and unusual to me I really started making mental notes of who showed up on the side of The Club. In other words, I paid attention to who was paying attention to the case. Custody cases are very rarely reported in the news unless the parents are celebrities. The witnesses are typically people like schoolteachers, neighbors, family members, medical personnel, and counselors. Grandparents usually testify what a great parent their own child is to the grandchild. In the case of Ex, he didn't have these family witnesses because the granddaddy had killed the grandmother.

The day care workers were there, however, to testify about the French kissing they witnessed when Ex dropped Gee off. And Ex's character witnesses were The Clan of the Frogmen, who had gathered around the sweat lodge with the little boy in attendance. And of course, there was the "random" woman on the train from Chicago who testified. The female psychologist (I'll call her Dr. See) was a member of MENSA and testified on behalf of Ex to say what a great dad he was. She also tried to make the point that he wasn't really a pedophile who was molesting his daughter. She was certain of that because she'd had sex with Ex before Ex and Ele got married.

That was a fact the doctor had failed to reveal to Ele when she agreed to be Ele's maid of honor at the wedding. Dr. See also comforted Ele by advising the concerned mom when she sought advice from her best friend, "Don't worry, there's not really anything to worry about with incest." After all, she disclosed that she'd had sex with her uncle for several years during her own childhood, and "it was the best thing that ever happened for her." When these facts were reported to the American Psychological Association, Dr. See lost her credentials and license to practice as a therapist. She moved away from Midland shortly after the trial.

This particular custody case had people out in the hallway checking on how things were progressing. Maybe it's not unusual for family members or friends to be checking, but this case involving Gee was different. One of the people who was checking on the case was a lawyer named David Lindemood. Up until that time, I don't believe I had ever met him. Someone told me he worked in the trust department at one of the banks in Midland. This was curious to me. Why would a lawyer who had nothing to do with this field of practice and wasn't on the witness list be checking on the case involving Gee and her parents? It was another piece of the information to put on my mental shelf and move on. I was really trying to pay close attention, as there was so much going on and so much of it was bizarre.

Judge Rucker appointed a younger lawyer in town to represent the interests of Gee. Many experts (approximately nine) testified at the jury trial that they believed it would be in the best interest of Gee for Ex's parental rights to be terminated. About two or three others said they thought it was not good for the rights to be terminated. The questions were submitted to the jury as to whether to terminate the rights between the father and daughter. If the answer was no, they had to decide who should have primary custody. The judge in Texas decides the visitation schedule, even if the jury decides who should have primary custody.

The attorney for Gee reported to the jury that Gee had "recanted" her story about Daddy loading a revolver and inserting it into her vagina. This recantation came after Gee had told and described to multiple CPS workers that it had happened. The court-appointed attorney also stood before the jury in the final arguments and recommended that they not terminate the father's rights. He argued that the little girl loved her daddy and Daddy loved her. The lawyer said for them not to worry, that Judge Rucker would enter a final ruling that would protect Gee if they had any concerns.

The jury came back with a ruling following the recommendation of the lawyer appointed by Judge Rucker. The jury did not terminate Dad's rights. The jury did, however, rule in favor of Ele, naming her the sole managing conservator of Gee. As far as the judge's ruling for Gee's protection, Judge Rucker gave Ex the standard possession order: no supervision, no restrictions. He got all the overnight access that any other noncustodial parent gets. He even got thirty days of summer visitation with Gee.

Judge Rucker also ordered that Mom had to pick up Gee from Ex at the end of the visitation period. This ruling effectively kept Mom close to Dad within a very limited geographical radius of where Ex lived. In other words, if Mom tried to move away to get Gee away from Dad, she would have to pay the cost of traveling to Midland to get her daughter back. This ruling basically kept Ele trapped in the Midland area, very close to Ex, so he could exercise his visitation rights with his daughter.

There was no valid point of error to appeal this ruling by Judge Rucker. The visitation was totally within the judge's discretion. All I could do at this point was make note and carry on. However, this was just the beginning of my observations and awareness of things yet to be revealed about The Club.

PUZZLE PIECES

I invite you to weigh the contradictions, silences, and overlooked dangers as you consider how juries, judges, and entire communities handle child safety when the stakes couldn't be higher.

- How should we interpret Gee's recantation—when she had been consistent and adamant with multiple caseworkers regarding Daddy loading the gun and inserting it into her vagina?
- How could a child this young even fabricate such a story if she had not experienced it?
- What does Judge Rucker's ruling (awarding standard possession, overnight access, and thirty days of summer visitation) reveal about how he cared about Gee's safety?

- How "random" is this train passenger who later attended the grandmother's funeral and testified as a character witness for Ex? Is it possible she was the same random woman who placed the phone call on the video Ex had filmed?
- What does the presence of two suspicious deaths (a murder and a reported suicide with no apparent investigation) suggest about the circle around Ex?
- Why did the psychologist who testified for Ex think that her personal sexual relationship with him would cancel the possibility that he was abusing his daughter?
- How might the motel room swap and other mind games affect a parent's ability to protect their child and participate effectively in litigation?

Chapter 5

PATTERNS

National research and government reviews repeatedly highlight common vulnerabilities in supervised visitation programs—underfunding, part-time or volunteer staff, variable security, and gaps in training and documentation.[1]

Sometime after my case wrapped up for Ele, an organization called Centers for Children and Families began doing the supervised visitations in family court for Midland and Odessa. According to the organization's LinkedIn bio and other sources, they have been around since 1957.[2] According to the secretary of state, the 501(c) corporation was established in 1959.[3] People working in the legal field generally refer to it as Centers.

This organization has two primary aspects. The Kids First program of the organization is set up to oversee supervised visitations for parents who are ordered by the court to use the facility for their visits with their children. The second part of Centers is the counseling side, where anyone needing a counselor can voluntarily go and obtain therapeutic help. It is also available for court-ordered counseling, should the judge decide to enter such an order. The majority of family law cases in Midland come through the 318th Judicial District Courts. Therefore, the majority of the court-ordered referrals to Centers in Midland came from Judge Dean Rucker.[4] It was a great concept, and many cities around Texas have similar organizations providing supervised visitation.

The protocol for supervised visitation at Centers is the custodial parent brings the child or children to the Centers location and leaves the child there while the noncustodial parent who needs to be supervised has their visit with the child or children. Usually, the visits are two hours long. Then the custodial parent comes and gets the child or children.

Centers has a board of directors comprising a reputable group of local citizens. They hold themselves out as hiring well-qualified, well-trained, and safe professionals to run the program for the visitation periods. They have "trained" monitors who videotape the sessions and remain in the room while the supervised parent is in the room with the child or children. If the lawyer wants a copy of the video session, they merely have to subpoena it and purchase the DVD (in former years) or flash drive (now). Centers has an office in Midland and another one in Odessa.

In 2011, I was working on two separate cases that both required Centers to conduct supervised visitations for the opposing side. On each of these cases, we discovered disturbing failures on the part of Centers and their personnel and methods.

CASE 1

In the first case, I was representing some grandparents who had custody of their grandchildren because both parents were meth addicts. These grandparents had spent time with the director of the Kids First program, Carol Taylor, getting assurances from her regarding the safety of their grandchildren. She told the grandparents she had military experience serving in the Marines. She assured them the monitors were well trained, and some were people from her church. However, the videos from the visits depicted violations of Centers's own rules and gaps in supervision. The videos didn't match the written reports in those sessions, which were being given a rating of "10," or excellent. The grandparents were concerned that the supervision was very inadequate.

I decided to take the deposition of the director. When I looked at her subpoenaed resume, she hardly had the qualifications one would expect for this position. She had not completed high school and had only a GED. Despite her claims, she had not been in the military at all. When I asked what church she attended, she made it clear that she did *not* attend a church anywhere. When I asked for the name of the monitor who had been in the room during the visits, she refused to give me their name, taking the position that their identity was confidential and I was harassing them to ask. The following is the redacted letter regarding these grandparents' experience with Centers.

May 17, 2012
XXXXXXXXXXX
XXXXXXXXXXX
Odessa, Texas XXXXX
Re: Centers for Children and Families, Kids First

To whom it may concern,
On January 11, of last year (2011), it became apparent to us that our daughter, XXXXXXXXXX, and the children's father, XXXXXXXXXX, had a serious methamphetamine drug and

drinking problem. It was to the point of endangering the lives of the children and neglect. We had to take them to court, and my wife was given temporary custody of the boys. During this process, we were introduced to the Kid's First program at Centers for Children and Families. At the time, we were ecstatic. The Kid's First Program seemed like a gift from God. It seemed to be exactly what we were looking for: supervised visitation schedules, someone to check the drug tests to ensure that visiting parent was negative for drugs, overall protection for the grandkids, a shield from unnecessary risk and stress, and an environment suitable for the kids to visit with their parents (if the parents were drug and alcohol free).

Little did we know that this program was going to be one of the worst nightmares that we have ever encountered. It started with the initial intake visit with Carol Taylor, Kids First Director, on March 30, 2011. During the visit, Carol Taylor acted like we were the enemy, explaining and going over the Kids First rules to us. Then she explained that "this was her playpen, she makes the rules and everyone has to follow her rules."

The court orders stated that XXXXXXXXXXXXX were to take monthly drug tests and provide the test results to Kids First, Carol Taylor. Since the very beginning, Carol Taylor has allowed at least six visitations when the visiting parent did not have a drug test and/or had tested positive for methamphetamine. This was exactly what we were trying to keep the kids away from. The kids want to see their parents, but not when the parents are on drugs. These visits had a negative effect on our grandchildren.

The visitations are set up with a monitor from Kids First supposedly documenting the entire session by using a video camera and taking notes. The Kids First program has a set of rules for the visiting parents to follow, which are to be enforced by the monitors. These rules are set to protect the kids. We have had to go to court to get copies of these video DVDs, even though the rules state that we have a right to get copies of these videos for a $20.00 fee. Before going to court, our attorney took Carol Taylor's and Hollie Carter's depositions. During the initial interview with Carol Taylor, she stated to us that she had been in the Marines, and she had learned a lot from them. She also bragged to our attorney's secretaries about her experience and what she had learned while she was in the Marine Corp and about her education. During her deposition, she changed her story and said that she never had been in the Marines, and she only had a high school GED. Holli Carter did have some college education, but her previous experience was selling hot dogs at a road side mobile hot dog cart on the highway and cleaning bars at night. We were really expecting to have someone with educational backgrounds and experience handling the kids.

We have reviewed the visitation video DVDs and were shocked at the rules being allowed to be broken by the kids' father. Also, there are gaps in the videos. The visitations sessions are for two hours. On one visit, the kids were in one room for a few minutes, and then they switched rooms for no apparent reason. There was <u>one hour and fifteen minutes missing</u> on that video during that session. We were so concerned that we hired a professional counselor with a Master's

Degree, Mr. Bill Ervin, to meet with the kids and to review the videos. He had great concerns with the way the visitation meetings were going. His letter is attached.

Carol Taylor told us during the initial interview that the monitors mostly came from her church. But during her deposition, she stated under oath that she "did not go to church." The monitors were not picked by her and that she did not know what qualified anyone to be a monitor, other than they were volunteers. Centers and Kids First will not show us any of the monitor's names, qualifications, history, or provide us with any background on them. This really bothers us. How can we honestly leave our grandkids with people that we know nothing about, and we do not know if the volunteers have any background criminal history or a history of pedophilia? We are being told by the people at Centers, Kids First to trust them concerning the monitors, yet we haven't always been told the truth by them.

On one visitation, the monitor's notes showed concern that the kid's father was still neglecting the middle child even after one-half of the visitation was over, yet she still gave the father a nine out of ten rating on the visitation. On another visitation, our three year old grandson needed to go to the bathroom. <u>The monitor decided to take our three year old grandson to the bathroom instead of letting his older brother take him.</u> This left the parent alone with the other two grandsons unsupervised in the room. Not only were they unsupervised, the monitor was working two visitations between the two rooms, so the other visitation went totally unsupervised while he was gone. Without knowing who the supervisors are or their background histories, I really do not want them taking my three year old grandson to the bathroom alone.

We first believed that the Centers and Kids First was a blessing come true. Yet with all the lies, broken rules, unprofessional conduct, and all of the deceitful dishonesty, we now wish that we had not asked the judge to use the program for our grandkids and certainly do pray that they do not receive funding in the future.

Sincerely,
XXXXXXXXXXXXXXX
XXXXXXXXXXXXXXX

CASE 2

In this second case, I was hired by a mother of twin girls. Their dad could see them only by having supervised visitations at Centers. The mom noticed the girls seemed to be traumatized by the visits, so she took them to one of the counselors at Centers. This counselor assured her that the girls were safe and she should trust that the supervised visits were properly monitored. Mom didn't think so even though the written reports coming from the director of Kids First were saying the visits were great and Dad was getting ratings of "10" on the reports.

Mom obtained the DVDs and watched all of them, or at least what she could, since some of the DVDs had long gaps and missing portions. We wrote to Centers requesting they provide us a complete video of the most disturbing session. Although we repeatedly requested, we never got the full two-hour recording. Nevertheless, what we got and what we showed the judge in court demonstrated

Dad having the two girls on the floor on their backs with Dad on top of them, in a sort of push-up position. He was kissing them back and forth, repeatedly saying, "kissy, kissy" over sixty times on just one of the supervised visits. He was also grinding his pelvic area into the two girls' private areas. He sniffed their armpits and crotches and asked if they washed their bottoms.

This case was an Odessa lawsuit being heard by Judge Denn Whalen of the 70th Judicial District Court. On March 26, 2012, at the end of the trial and after watching this video, Judge Whalen ruled that this dad would never have any visitation with these girls again. He also had Dad hauled out of the courtroom in handcuffs and off to jail for contempt for nonpayment of some medical bills. Dad's red BMW sat in the parking lot at the courthouse for a few days before someone picked it up. Dad stayed in jail for sixty days, serving his sentence for contempt of court.

Excerpt from the testimony of this case involving the twin girls is as follows:

THE COURT: Raise your right hand, please.
CAROL TAYLOR,
Having been first duly sworn, testified as follows:

DIRECT EXAMINATION
BY MR. BARRERA:

Q. Ms. Taylor, would you please state your name for the record.

A. Carol Lynn Taylor.

Q. And, Ms. Taylor, what is your position?

A. I work for Centers for Children and Family. I'm the director of the Kids First program.

Q. How long have you been the director of Kids First?

A. I want to say about three years.

Q. Okay. And can you tell us what the scores were of his visitations by the observers?

A. On an average, sir, they were a ten, except on the one with the intervention.

Q. And what was that scoring on the intervention?

A. Nine.

Q. And what is nine or a ten mean one the Centers' criteria?

A. From eight to 10 it's considered a good visit.

CROSS EXAMINATION
BY MS. CLACK:

Q. Ma'am, we have a very short amount of time.

A. Yes, ma'am.

Q. But you were subpoenaed to be here at 1:30 today; is that correct?

A. Yes, ma'am.

Q. Were you here at 1:30 when Dr. Kristin Jensen testified?

A. Yes, ma'am.

Q. You heard her entire testimony; is that correct?

A. Yes, ma'am, I did.

Q. Now, you heard that she was highly disturbed by what she saw taking place at Centers?

A. Yes, ma'am.

Q. You heard that, right?

A. I sure did.

Q. Now, she has a PhD and some 28 years of experience with sex offenders and so forth, right?

A. Yes.

Q. You also heard her testimony about reviewing the report of Dr. Beaty, another psychologist out of the Dallas area, who is highly concerned and offended about what was going on in your organization over there at Centers; you've heard that, too, right?

A. I heard it, yes.

Q. Ma'am, the highest level of education you have achieved, according to your resume, which is part of Petitioner's Exhibit 2, is that you have a GED?

A. That is correct.

Q. Okay. So, basically, you did not finish high school; is that right?

A. Yes.

Q. Okay. Now, you're here in charge of the supervised visitation for protecting the children who are sent by the judges out here in West Texas for supervised visitation. You're the director of that program; is that true?

A. Yes.

Q. Now, ma'am, you also heard, within this Petitioner's Exhibit 2, you've seen this letter, have you not?

A. Yes.

Q. That was sent to Centers?

A. Yes.

Q. To both Ann Bradford and Carolyn Gregory, complaining about the fact that you have missing parts from the January 15, 2011, visit?

A. Yes.

Q. And I have correctly stated, have I not, all of our efforts to try to get copies of that DVD?

A. Yes.

Q. That those statements within this letter are true and correct, isn't that true?

A. Yes.

Q. Okay. And so you have provided me with three separate sets of DVDs, each of them defective, each of them with missing parts of that January 15, 2011, visit, isn't that true?

A. Yes.

Q. And so what . . . there was a person by the name of Mary who signed off on that particular visit. She was your video operator, and she was also the person responsible for keeping those children safe when Daddy was sniffing their crotch, sniffing under their arms, and getting on top of them. You heard that from Dr. Kristin Jensen, isn't that true?

A. I heard her say that.

Q. And Mary gave him a rating of 10 as a great visit, isn't that true?

A. Mary gave him a ten.

Q. Okay. And you had access to that videotape for a year to see whether there were concerns, did you not, ma'am?

A. Yes.

Q. And you were at Centers, the same organization where Mary Biggs has been seeing these children, counseling with these children, talking about how disturbed these children are by their visits with Dad and all of his kissy, kissy behavior. You've also had access within your own organization to be aware of those children's concerns, are you not?

A. From Mary Biggs, ma'am.

Q. Ma'am, within your organization, attached to this letter, Mary Biggs has been reporting that the children have been having problems with Mr. Pesquiera, isn't that true?

A. I don't have access to Mary Biggs files, ma'am.

Q. Okay. It's within your organization?

A. It's in my organization.

Q. So Ann Bradford had access to the—

A. She should.

Q. And she's, basically, your boss over there?

A. She is.

Q. Okay. So within your organization you had the information how these children were being damaged by these supervised visits that you were in charge of, isn't that true?

A. Yes.

Q. And so, as we sit here today, your supervisors call it a ten, and Dr. Jensen calls it a—dangerous and don't ever let this man be alone with these children. Is there quite a contrast between Mary's analysis and Dr. Jensen's analysis?

A. Yes.

Q. And where do you fall in the analysis? Have you watched these videos?

A. I watched them some time ago. I did not see the smelling of the crotch that you indicate. So I wouldn't feel comfortable saying that.

Q. Are you ready to watch what he was doing? Do you want to—is that because you say it didn't happen?

A. I'm not saying it didn't happen, ma'am. I'm saying that I do not recall that.

Q. Did you watch every bit of every one of these videos?

A. I watched them a long time ago, ma'am. And I have lots of videos that I watch.

Q. When you sent me the first set of videos, you knew that 30 minutes was missing from that first video, did you not?

A. No. That's what I was going to explain.

Q. Okay. So you watched it—you watched something that had more on the video tape than what you sent me, isn't that true?

A. I believed I watched the whole video, ma'am.

Q. Well, you know how long the time—

A. I didn't take the time—I didn't measure the time or take the time on it. I believed I watched an entire video, ma'am.

Q. Well, you wrote me a rather sharp letter telling me that you had sent it and you weren't going to send it again.

A. I can be sharp, but I'm not quite sure if I was that sharp with you.

Q. Okay. It was only when I kept referencing that I had experts pointing out that there was missing time and we have very disturbing conduct going on, being depicted, that you sent me another one.

A. I think I've sent you three copies, ma'am.

Q. And every one of them has been different, isn't that true?

A. I do not know. I have not seen them.

Q. Well, in preparation for today's hearing, did you go back and watch any of these videos recently?

A. I've been out of the state for—

Q. Is that a no?

A. No.

REDIRECT EXAMINATION
BY MR. BARRERA:

Q. Would you like to see the video?

A. No.

Q. No?

A. No, sir.

THE COURT: The Court would like to see that.

MS. CLACK: Okay.

THE COURT: Okay. The Court makes the following ruling, after having previously ruled on the Movant's Motion to Compel. With respect to the Motion to Modify, the Court finds that there have been material and substantial changes with respect to the parties and the children, the subjects of this suit, since we renditioned the final decree of divorce that was entered August 20, 2007.

I fully expected to come in here today and grant you visitation with these two children, but I've just been completely and totally compelled by the, not only the testimony that I've heard, the video that I've heard, and quite frankly, your testimony, Mr. Pesquiera, that the Court's going to air [sic]on the side of safety for these children. And I'm going to order that you have no contact with these children until further order of this Court. And that means none. Nothing. No letters. No telephonic. Nothing. Nothing. And it's rendered effective this date.

The executive director of Centers, Ann Bradford (wife of Midland County Judge Mike Bradford), was present in court the day that Judge Whalen ruled. Her position was that Centers had done a great job and that her director of the Kids First program had done a great job. I didn't agree. Judge Whalen didn't agree.

I wrote a letter to the board of directors of Centers urging that they investigate these disturbing facts and matters regarding the lack of credentials for the director of the Kid's First program and the gaps in the videos. Their lawyer wrote back to me on April 10, 2012, and told me not to contact them again except through him.

I never heard anything further regarding any investigation at Centers or addressing my concerns. As of June 27, 2025, Bradford is still shown as the registered agent for Centers with the Texas secretary of state. Definitely, I was seeing some patterns. I needed to keep watching.

PUZZLE PIECES

The following questions are designed to help you think critically about the safeguards and failures in supervised visitation.

- Why would Midland County's supervised visitation program hire a person to head up the program when she was so clearly lacking in qualifications?
- Why was she kept on staff when it was revealed that she had lied about her credentials?
- Why did Centers refuse to reveal the names of the monitors who were in the room?

- Why were the monitors who were in the room allowing the father to get on top of the little girls and sniff their crotches?
- Why were the administrators, employees, and volunteers allowing these children to be abused on camera and then giving the father the highest rating possible as a good visit?
- Was this ignorance, stupidity, or a pattern of protection for predators being carried out at Centers in Midland, Texas?
- Were these two cases random examples of incompetence, or do you think they are part of an actual pattern of grooming and abuse at the very location and organization that was intended to protect children?
- How important was it that the mother requested, paid for, and watched every single video recorded session?

Chapter 6

PROTECTING THE PREDATORS

A recent study analyzing how courts handle abuse and alienation claims notes that courts believed less than a quarter of claims that a father has committed child physical or sexual abuse.[1]

Over the years of my law practice, I have realized the importance of paying attention not only to what people say but to what they do. When I meet a potential client for the first time, I usually schedule the appointment for an hour and a half. I learn a whole lot of things about them during this ninety-minute consultation. Before they walk into my office, my staff has already written down the basic information: age, the number of children and their ages, their place of employment, annual salary, etc. Obviously, this person has come to seek my advice and to determine whether they want to hire me on some current or upcoming litigation. I am also asking questions of the potential client to get a grasp of what the real issues are in my opinion.

During my career, I have probably represented an equal number of male clients and female clients. I am amazed at the men who come into my office for the first consult and what they say about their wives: They'll say, "She's a great mother" and then tell me about her affair, the filthy house, and her attempted suicide in recent months. His wife may say she loves the child, and she may have nursed the child as a baby, but this man is not describing the conduct and actions of a "good" mother by my definition. As we visit further, I begin to realize that this man really doesn't think she was a good mother at all, but he just doesn't have the confidence or hope to realize that a man could win a custody battle with these kinds of facts. Yes, it could be expensive in terms of legal fees, and it could take a while, but it is possible for a father to win a custody case with these kinds of facts.

There are also the women who come to me and say their husbands love them, but they are in a controlling relationship in which the husbands keep them on a strict budget for groceries, though the man has plenty of money for his extracurricular activities, such as golf, alcohol, affairs, sex toys, drugs, and the like.

These various descriptions that I hear from potential clients at the first consultation help me tremendously to know what we are really dealing with. Obviously, this person is facing litigation or thinking about it, or else they wouldn't be sitting in my office consulting with me about a divorce or custody battle. When we add to the basic facts that this person may have given up a career to be the stay-at-home parent, they are facing additional issues to be considered. The husband may be the one consulting with me and feels trapped having to work long hours and overtime while the wife (whom he just called a "good mom") stays home stoned on marijuana or prescription meds. People in these situations feel trapped, angry, scared, and lost. Many of them have been lied to, betrayed, gaslighted, and abused. The abuse might be physical, but sometimes it is emotional, psychological, financial, and/or verbal.

My experience has taught me many things about human beings and their relationships with one another. I am constantly learning, even to this day. In paying attention to judges, the learning curve is no different. These people who put on the judicial robe and sit in front of the courtroom presiding over cases are lawyers who were either elected or appointed to the position. Some of them are people of integrity and high moral character; others are not. After all, they are human beings, just like the rest of us. All of us have made mistakes, missing the mark to say the right thing or take the proper action. I think we can all agree that every human being on earth is a work in progress. Each of us has the opportunity to wake up to a new day (God willing) and choose our path. We can choose a path of wrongdoing, or we can choose a path that embraces good choices and good decisions.

Lawyers are required to attend continuing education courses and seminars as a part of holding and maintaining a law license. The subject matter of these speeches and lectures can be on a variety of topics. Since I am board certified in family law by the Texas Board of Legal Specialization, the seminars I attend usually deal with updates on the legislation involving family law matters, appellate court rulings interpreting the laws and trial court rulings, ethics, evidence, experts, discovery, trial tactics, trial techniques, office management, and so on. Sometimes the speakers are judges and panels of judges.

I pay particular attention when one of the judges I practice in front of is speaking at one of these seminars because what they say can reveal valuable information. Sometimes these judges tell the attendees what they like and don't like in technique, style, and presentation. Sometimes they reveal what impresses them in the courtroom.

These tidbits of insight are important because we lawyers are not supposed to be too close to a judge we practice law before, or it starts giving the impression of impropriety. Hearing from a judge in a group setting is considered more proper. Private meetings and friendships might raise an eyebrow in terms of questioning whether the lawyers had some form of ex parte communication with the judge. This means it is completely against the code of ethics for a judge and a lawyer to have communication with one another without both parties' lawyers present if the discussion is about a case that is pending before that judge. The foundation of our trust in the legal system is that we have laws and that they are ethically followed and enforced. When lawyers and judges fail to respect and follow the basic rules of ethics and the other rules of law, we start seeing cracks in the legal system. When this happens, we begin to doubt our judicial system, and the trust in the whole system begins to crumble.

Judges need to be fair and honest and know the law. And they need to apply the law in a manner that is just. Every judge I've ever known to address the subject of children has said that they are in favor of protecting children from abuse. They give speeches and lectures and participate in panel discussions at these seminars talking about children being their priority, but that's not always what they do in the courtroom with their rulings.

In 2010, I was representing a mother of a little girl who was six years old. The parents were divorced and lived in Midland. The dad had standard visitation. Mom was taking the little girl to a woman named Charlotte Starr, a professional counselor who had developed the Effective Parenting program for families and children.

Charlotte was a woman who had years of classroom experience as a teacher and had retired from public schools. She was a professional reading specialist and a certified kindergarten and elementary school teacher. She worked with parents who wanted to give their child an extra bit of help with a multitude of issues facing families these days. She had testified multiple times in the Midland County Courts for preadoption home studies. Her resume stated she had testified approximately 120 times. I had several clients over the years who had used Charlotte's services, and I always heard rave reviews of how much her advice and suggestions helped them and their children.

Charlotte testified in court on parenting issues and the nuances in families that were relevant to custody and visitation decisions. One day, while working with my client and her six-year-old daughter, the little girl told Charlotte that she was cold when she slept at Daddy's because she didn't wear pajamas. She slept naked with Daddy, who was also naked. The little girl also revealed that her feet tickled his private parts while they were in bed.

Obviously, this revelation by the little girl was something Charlotte was required to report to Child Protective Services (CPS), so she did. The CPS worker did her interviews and investigation. I filed for a protective order and a Petition to Modify the father's visitation rights and asked the court to either suspend his time with the daughter or put him on supervised visitation.

The Court of Continuing Jurisdiction was the 318th Judicial District, presided by Judge Dean Rucker. We had our temporary hearing seeking emergency relief. Mom testified about her concerns. Charlotte testified as to what the little girl revealed and her concerns. The CPS worker testified. Dad testified and admitted that he was sleeping in the nude with his six-year-old daughter and that she was sleeping in the nude.

When the hearing was over, Judge Dean Rucker did not stop Dad's visitation or put him under any supervision. In fact, he denied the protective order in its entirety. He addressed Dad and told him not to sleep naked with his daughter. The judge announced his court order in a letter to the lawyers dated April 18, 2011, that fired Starr. But it didn't stop there. He also ordered that my client was enjoined from taking the little girl to Starr ever again for any reason.

PUZZLE PIECES

- How does firing a well-regarded professional counselor for testifying raise concerns about silencing credible witnesses?
- Is this case an example of a judge ruling in the best interest of the little girl?
- Why would a judge not be disturbed by a father sleeping in the nude with his six-year-old daughter who was also nude and touching his genital area with her feet?
- What questions do you have about this ruling by Judge Rucker?
- What is this puzzle we are piecing together beginning to look like to you?

Chapter 7

SEX TRAFFICKING IN MIDLAND

Today, there are 49.6 million people in modern slavery worldwide, and 12 million of them are children. Fifty-four percent of those trapped in modern slavery are women and girls.[1]

On June 21, 2012, I met a woman named Karen. She had scheduled a divorce consult with me. When I reviewed her intake information, I noticed she and her husband, Mike, had been married for thirty-four years. They had three grown children and owned a local art gallery and frame shop that had been in business for twenty-seven years. On paper, everything looked perfect.

However, when we started talking, I began to learn why Karen was needing a divorce. She had stumbled across some disturbing information on the computer at the art gallery. She discovered her husband was living a secret life in which he was communicating with women on a website called ECCIE. Our research revealed this was an acronym for Escort Client Community Information Exchange. The women Mike was interacting with on this website were sex workers. In addition to communicating with them, he was having sex with them and paying them thousands of dollars for their services.

But it didn't stop there. These women were flying and driving into Midland, Texas, from various parts of the country and staying at the downtown DoubleTree by Hilton hotel. According to the chats on ECCIE, Mike was coordinating appointments with other local men so they could have their time with these women who were being trafficked to Midland.

Karen shared the printouts from the gallery's computer showing the evidence of Mike's activities with these women. He used the code name "TexasBrowning." She also shared that the men were called Hobbyists, and the women were called Providers. These Hobbyists and Providers had their flirtatious exchanges right there on the ECCIE website. Karen was furious that these prostitutes were flirting with her husband and having sex with him. She was also furious that he was paying them thousands of dollars for their services. She was shocked, humiliated, and angry.

Part of the rules of this ECCIE Club was that the men had to acquire and use a cell phone dedicated only to this purpose of communicating with the Providers and the other Hobbyists. This was not to be the cell phone for the family plan, where a guy's wife or kids could discover it. Obviously, it was to be something like a TracFone or burner phone. Mike kept his Hobby phone locked up in his gun vault with his very large expensive gun collection and ammunition. When Karen and Mike built their house, Mike had designed this safe and secure room inside their garage. He kept it locked, yet he occasionally allowed visitors over to show them his impressive gun collection. Karen stated that one of these visitors was Midland County Judge Mike Bradford—husband of Ann Bradford, the executive director of Centers, an organization you may recall from chapter 5. He had arrived with two men from Las Vegas, Nevada, who had also wanted to see the guns in the gun room. My opinion of the people coming to look at the gun room and its contents was that this behavior was a little off. Most of the people I know who own a lot of guns are very private about it. They keep them locked away and don't disclose their whereabouts. As a part of the divorce process, when it came to making the gun room and its contents available to my licensed federal firearms dealer for the purpose of inventorying and placing a value on the guns and ammo for the required Inventory and Appraisement for court, we didn't get that same open-door availability and hospitality.

In addition to Karen's husband having a Hobby phone with the Providers' phone numbers, he also had the other participating men, the Hobbyists, in that phone listed with their code names and their phone numbers. The other men used names like "ne1469Hot Rod," "Twain," "Mdtexguy," "Rick," "Ray McKigney," "delimex007," "Johnnybax," "Shep3.0," "robinhood12," "Big Tex77," and "Z10." At the first hearing, on July 11, 2012, before Judge Rucker, Karen's husband admitted to being on the ECCIE website, although he initially acted as though he didn't know who "TexasBrowning" was. The lawyers at the first hearing were two men from Attorney Hal Brockett's office, one of them being David Lindemood. A copy of that testimony reads as follows:

CROSS-EXAMINATION
BY: MS. CLACK:

Q. Sir, you've had a chance to—for the last few minutes to go over Petitioner's Exhibit Number 2 with your lawyers. Is that correct?
Explain position [*sic*]—
(Pause)

A. No, I have not seen that.

Q. Well, that top page there, that's from your website. Is that not your e-mail? You're Mike at—[redacted]?

A. I am Mike at [redacted], yes.

Q. And you sign off as TB. Is that right?

A. It looks like it, yes.

Q. And that's because you use the name Texas Browning. Isn't that right?

A. For what?

Q. For the Eccie website. You used it there in connection with [redacted]. Isn't that right?

A. It looks like I put it down, yes.

Q. Okay. Because you use the name Texas Browning, don't you?

A. I don't know Texas Browning. Who is that?

Q. Sir, you are saying that you've never been on a website called Eccie, E-C-C-I—

A. I'm familiar with it.

Q. Okay. And you've been on it, have you not?

A. I've seen it, yes, ma'am.

Q. And you have written on it, have you not?

A. I have seen it, yes, ma'am.

Q. And you have brought gals in here called providers into Midland, and you've had sex with them, have you not?

A. They are actually provided as escorts, ma'am.

Q. Sir, you've had sex with women that have—brought in from that Eccie website. Isn't that true?

A. I've been with a few women, yes, ma'am.

Q. You have had sex with them. Is that right?

A. I have been with a few women, yes, ma'am.

THE COURT: Answer the question, sir.

Q. (By Ms. Clack) And you have rated them on this Eccie website, have you not?

A. It's been a while.

Q. Well, what? A month?

A. It's been a while.

Q. You were up in—

A. I don't remember, ma'am.

Q. You were up in Tulsa in recent weeks with one of these women, have you—

A. No, ma'am, I have not been in Tulsa.

THE COURT: Let Ms. Clack finish her question before you respond, sir.

THE WITNESS: Oh, excuse me.

Q. (By Ms. Clack) Sir, you have not—you are swearing under oath you have not been in Tulsa in recent week?

A. Yes, ma'am, I am.

Q. In—excuse me—Oklahoma City?

A. I had business in Oklahoma City, yes, ma'am.

Q. Okay. And part of your business in Oklahoma City was having sex with one of these women. Isn't that true?

A. I went to Prix de West, art business. Prix de West is a by-invitation-only art show at the—

Q. Sir—

A. —Western Heritage Museum.

MS. CLACK: Objection, non-responsive.

Q. (By Ms. Clack) Sir, did you—

THE COURT: Sustained. Listen to the question and answer the question, sir.

Q. (By Ms. Clack) Did you have sex with a woman other than your wife while you were in Oklahoma City?

A. No, ma'am.

Q. Sir, you have paid up to $1,500.00 for sexual favors from these women—from some of these women. Isn't that true?

A. No, ma'am.

Q. You've paid up to $1,300.00 with some of these women. Isn't that true?

A. The—no, ma'am.

THE WITNESS: May I divulge more information, Your Honor?

MR. LINDEMOOD: Answer the question.

THE COURT: Answer the question, sir.

Q. (By Ms. Clack) These are called fees on that ECCIE website, aren't they?

A. I think they're called donations.

Q. Okay. So when you give these donations, you have donated to these gals' airfare. Isn't that true?

A. Not necessarily.

Q. Well, sometimes?

A. It's been a few years.

Q. You have charged on a credit card to bring some of these women into Midland. Isn't that true?

A. Yes.

Q. And you have spent thousands of dollars over these years toward these—these providers. Isn't that true?

A. Over the last few years.

Q. And sometimes as much—over $5,000.00 within a three-day period. Isn't that true?

A. I don't think so.

Q. Well, you don't recall when you had somebody named Amanda and Tiffany, and you had the menage a trois that's talked about in Petitioner's Exhibit 2? Do you remember paying them $13.00 [*sic*] each and having two different sessions with them in March a year ago?

A. I haven't had the opportunity to look at this, ma'am.

Q. Well, I'm just asking your memory. Don't you remember the two women that you had sex with together for the $1,300.00 each?

MR. LINDEMOOD: Judge, I object on the basis of relevance at this point in a temporary hearing.

THE COURT: Overruled. It will go to the weight. Answer the question.

A. It's been a few years ago.

Q. (By Ms. Clack) But you do remember it, don't you?

A. Vaguely, yes.

The ECCIE website showed Mike to have a join date of March 31, 2010, as "TexasBrowning." His posts had also shown up as "Guest061612-1." The reason we knew this was Mike's new code name was because not only did his new posts show him as "Guest061612-1," but all of the old posts of "TexasBrowning" now showed up as "Guest061612-1." He would also like to refer to himself in some of his posts as "The Texas Legend Continues."

Our investigators were just watching the weird comedy of not-so-clever chatter. What we were also seeing was that my client's husband was the one taking a leadership role in lining up the women to come to Midland, Texas, and then encouraging the other men by saying things like "If we don't schedule these appointments, we aren't going to keep getting these quality women coming to Midland." The following are some of "TexasBrowning"/"Guest061612-1" posts:

07-17-2010, 5:35 PM TexasBrowning posted: "Okay Ladies bring some of your VIP touches out here to West Texas. We have not been hit nearly as bad as say Dallas or Houston. In fact, we have the lowest un-employment in the state. Everybody is working so we can afford you high class ladies. I just wish more of you would visit us."

08-28-2010, 1:20 PM TexasBrowning posted: "PLEASE CUM to West Texas, Midland to be exact. We are not nearly as affected by the nation's bad economy. ASK ANY OF THE VIP PROVIDERS that have come to Midland in the last month or so. employers are hiring as fast as they can find good people, and that relates to lots of money on the streets. AND; most important to the VIP PROVIDERS, the VIP "Gentlemen" probably have more money right now, than they ever had . . . check it out on your own and cum see ME."

09-15-2010 at 4:31 PM TexasBrowning AKA Mike posted: "Cum the 1st week of October . . . better for me at least. Midland has a lot of GENTLEMEN VIPS, that prefer to stay downtown, so they can just walk down the street like they are going to another office but stop off for a "tour." I for one recceomend [sic] the Midland Hilton right downtown. It may cost a little more but it is very secure, and clean, and they have a parking garage . . . If you are interested email me back, and I will help if I can . . . just cum see me! With your "Assets" you should do well."

01-12-2011, 11:48 AM Chica Chaser commented to a TexasBrowning Post: "*Excellent! Good recruiting work.*"

01-12-2011, 12:11 PM TexasBrowning posted: "Thanks . . . she is a jewel. I have a lot of VIP stuff like this, or believe it or not better. They are willing to come to Midland . . . however; just for me or you or whomever to get them here, they want either a 3 or 4 hour commitment. Then the rest of the guys get to enjoy the remainder of the time they are here. OK; here's my question to all you hard Dicks . . . If I start inviting these ladies . . . can we take turns ponying up the four hour tours, so we can all have some VIP fun. Mandy came out; I picked her up at the airport, went to her place on the 6th floor, and I donated 1500 for four hours, then the rest of you enjoyed shorter term dates . . ."

03-08-11 at 2:43 PM TexasBrowning posted: "Ok gentlemen . . . Amanda is in Midland as you read this. She will be in here until Friday. Tiffany Europe will be here tonight and will stay until Friday. Please help me in welcoming two of the most beautiful sexiest women you will ever lay eyes on. I get em [*sic*] here but you have to make appointments . . . Ok; the rest is up to you."—TexasBrowning

He gave "Amanda Taylor" and "Tiffany Europe's" contact info.

The following is a post that Mike made eight months before Karen stumbled upon his illegal activities and lifestyle:

> 09-15-2011, 1:15 PM TexasBrowning posted: "Recruit Gentlemen . . . Recruit. I have been doing it for a year and a half now. CC . . . remember how bad it was in 2009?"

The posts continued:

> 11-05-2011, 9:10 AM in regard to "Incredibly beautiful Piper is in Midland today" TexasBrowning posted: "Men of West Texas . . . We have a rare treat visiting us from Phoenix. A lot of you know me, and know I spend a lot of time recruiting providers to West Texas. Do yourself a favor, and gulp it down . . . See this beautiful woman and enjoy her. I had the pleasure of spending an entire evening with her last year . . . I get em [*sic*] to Midland . . . The rest is up to you. PS . . . I have her booked late Sunday night all night."

In all of this back-and-forth dialogue regarding the arrangements going on, there was another group of people in the mix. They were the Moderators. Their role, the best I could tell, was to monitor the dialogue and censor (redact) any words or phrases that might compromise the name of the hotel where the men would be meeting the Providers for their sexual encounters.

For example, one of the men named the hotel in his chat, but the monitor caught it and blacked out the name. It was obvious to all of us working on this divorce case that it was the Hilton hotel in downtown Midland, with an underground parking garage. Everyone from Midland and this area knows there is only one hotel downtown (the Midland DoubleTree by Hilton), and it has an underground parking garage. Whoever this censor was, they were *not* familiar with the one and only hotel in downtown Midland.

These Moderators also had their own handles when they were chatting on the ECCIE website. These people used the names "CryptKicker—Moderationg the Darkness" and "Chica Chaser—Administrator." Sometimes "Chica Chaser" was listed as "Super Moderator." There was also a person using the name of "Antichrist666" as their handle on the posts. Obviously, this was all illegal sex trafficking. This was not a solo streetwalker coming to Midland to "service" some high-powered businessmen. This was definitely organized criminal activity. Many people were involved in this criminal endeavor. We even looked at the pictures and profiles of various young women (mostly in their twenties) who were the Providers. There was even a glossary of terms describing what services and combinations of activities these women would perform.

Now that I have had a few years to think about what I was looking at in terms of what these young women were describing in what they could and would perform, it is apparent to me that we were not looking at a group of women who on their eighteenth birthday voluntarily decided to become an internet prostitute. And I don't think they learned these things from crawling into the back seat of the car and having sex with their boyfriend.

These women were groomed to fly and drive into a city and play the part: gushing over wealthy men in their fifties and sixties and telling them how wonderful and amazing these Hobbyists were. It appeared to me they were not only groomed to do all of this for men to pay thousands of dollars for their two- to three-hour slot of time, but they also had to have the help and coordination of many others. They had to have help and assistance from housekeeping at the hotel. It's only logical that someone had to be bringing in fresh towels and sheets in between appointments with the men. They had to have the knowledge and cooperation of someone within the management of the hotel. This was a time when hotels were staying full and no rooms were available. The cost for booking hotel rooms in Midland was at a premium, yet these women were coming in frequently. They were also setting up their business "tours" in the most expensive suites in the hotel, and it seemed these suites were readily available whenever they came.

Everything about the ECCIE website and Mike's conduct screamed of illegal activity. We calculated that, based upon the conversations and admissions through chat activity and the pricing lists printed on it, Karen's husband had spent at least $200,000 on prostitutes.

While working on the divorce case, we were trying to get valuations on the guns and ammo. We also needed to calculate the amount of money Mike spent defrauding the marital estate for his payments to the sex workers. Mike had hired Hal Brockett as his lawyer; however, Brockett did very little in regard to showing up for the depositions, which took place after the temporary hearing. The lawyer who did show up to represent Mike was David Lindemood, who was of counsel at Hal's office.

This divorce was one with quite a few hard-fought battles, from our perspective. The first hearing was held sixteen days after we filed the original petition for divorce. We were asking at the temporary orders hearing that the judge set the ground rules as to who would pay what bills and who would live in the house, as well as set temporary injunctions to not spend money on certain things, and so on. Most of the time, these hearings can be fairly routine, and everyone agrees to behave and keep things as status quo.

However, the circumstances leading up to Karen and Mike's

first hearing were not simple or ordinary. Only three days before we filed this divorce petition, Mike had purportedly sold the parties' family business, the art gallery, to a wealthy elderly woman named Ann Arick who lived next door to Karen and Mike's residence. He sold the business to her for $400,000, only a fraction of what Karen believed it was worth. In this quick and slick attempt by Karen's husband, he was going to cheat Karen out of her share of the community estate and property division. Karen filed for divorce on June 25, 2012. Ms. Arick wrote a check for $400,000 to Mike on June 22, 2012, which he deposited on June 22, 2012. The following is a purchase and sales agreement dated June 25, 2012, between Mike and Ms. Arick, along with a photo of Ms. Arick's home next door to Karen and Mike's house.

PURCHASE AND SALES AGREEMENT

This AGREEMENT is between [redacted] Michael [redacted] DBA [redacted] hereinafter called Seller, whose address is [redacted], Midland, Texas, [redacted] [redacted] [redacted] agrees to sell to Ann E. Arick, whose address is PO Box 87, Midland, Texas 79701, hereinafter called buyer, the assets of [redacted] as described below:

All art work owned by [redacted] including original art, paper and canvas prints, sculptures and accessories. All furniture and fixtures, shop equipment, framing supplies and associated materials.

Purchase Price: $400,000. (Four Hundred Thousand Dollars.)

Buyer agrees to assume sellers lease at [redacted] Midland TX [redacted] where [redacted] currently resides. [redacted] [redacted] offers to allow Buyer to continue using the [redacted] name and logo, website and paid in advance advertising.

Seller agrees to furnish Buyer with inventory of art on consignment and assist Buyer in continuing the contract with the artists, or, to return art to artist at Buyer's expense.

EXECUTED THE 25th DAY OF June, 2012

Ann E. Arick
BUYER (Ann E. Arick)

SELLER [redacted] Michael [redacted]

Mike [redacted] DBA [redacted] will be responsible for all monthly bills, sales taxes, Lease payments and associated payments for consigned sales through July 31, 2012.

Ann E. Arick will be responsible for the monthly bills, sales taxes, Lease payments and associated payments for consigned sales effective August 1, 2012.

Witnesed by: Randy Brown Date: 6/25, 2012

PETITIONER'S EXHIBIT 3 7-11-12

Arick was a multimillionaire from her oil royalty inheritance. She had no children to leave her vast wealth to. Interestingly, Karen's husband, Mike, was ultimately the one named in her last will and testament to receive her property upon her death in December 2016.

Before I even met Karen, she had scheduled an appointment with Brockett to consider having him be her divorce lawyer. Karen showed up at the scheduled time for her appointment. It was only upon arriving at Brockett's office that Karen was informed that Mr. Brockett could not consult with her because he had a conflict of interest. It was after that cancellation of her appointment with Mr. Brockett that Karen scheduled a consult with me.

When Karen came to her first appointment with me and laid out the description of their marital estate, the evidence of Mike's dealings with sex workers on the art gallery computer, and how he was conducting himself in a deceptive and criminal manner, I knew that this was going to be a difficult and probably long, protracted case. I quoted her a large retainer that she would need to pay before I signed on and began to file legal papers on her behalf.

This case was going to be in Judge Rucker's court. Based on my prior experiences in his court, I knew that I couldn't count on Judge Rucker to order Mike to pay me interim attorney's fees, or even attorney's fees at the conclusion of the case for that matter.

I had learned that lesson very well in 2011 when I won a jury verdict in a highly contested custody trial, which you will learn about in the next chapter. In that case, Rucker submitted the question to the jury, and they answered that the opposing side—the dad, who was a multimillionaire—should pay me $320,000 in attorney's fees. However, when he entered his final judgment, he denied the attorney's fees being paid to me and ordered that the dad pay nothing.

I had definitely learned the lesson after three decades of practicing law that I needed to get my retainer up front before I signed on to represent a client.

At the first hearing, Mike testified he had not paid anything to Brockett and his team of lawyers to begin representing him to appear in court at the first hearing. All kinds of questions were swirling through my head. Hal was considered one of the top family law attorneys in Midland. He had also been practicing law for about the same number of years as I had. I had lots of questions as to why Hal would sign on to such a complicated case with these kinds of issues for no up-front retainer.

In the course of my representation of Karen, we gathered up the evidence of the ECCIE website communications and the Hobby phone and met several times with Agent Sean Powers with the FBI. One of my investigators, Karen, and I also took the volumes of evidence to the Midland Police Department and met with their vice detective. We also turned over Mike's Hobby phone to the officer. We knew from following the dialogue initiated by "TexasBrowning"/"Guest061612-1," aka Mike, that he was discussing and facilitating the arrangements for one of the Providers to be coming to town in the next few days. We notified the Midland Police Department of the time and location of the appointments and waited for them to do something.

On August 28, 2012, Mike joined the ECCIE website as "45Colt." Later, his posts showed his handle as "110912." We knew this was Mike because of the fact that when he joined, his post showed "The Texas Legend Continues," same as when he was "TexasBrowning."

One of my licensed private investigators, Corby Eades, had connections with a friend in the Andrews, Texas, sheriff's office who also worked as a liaison with the FBI. When Corby turned over the evidence, he was told by his friend that "what we were dealing with was fifty times bigger than Ms. Clack imagined." The next day, we learned that FBI Agent Powers, with whom we had been dealing, had been transferred out of Midland. We never heard from him again. We also never heard from anyone in the FBI again. And the Midland Police Department never got back to us on the appointments Mike had coordinated with the Provider.

During Karen and Mike's divorce, we took several depositions. Lindemood was the lawyer who was present in the room, representing Mike, while my investigator, Corby, testified in a deposition about turning over evidence to the FBI. Corby was also the licensed firearms dealer I used to inventory and appraise the guns and ammunition owned by the parties.

Lindemood was also the lawyer from Brockett's office representing Mike when I took Mike's deposition on January 4, 2013. Lindemood was instructing Mike to invoke his Fifth Amendment rights not to incriminate himself to any questions that involved the following issues:

- Prostitution
- Promotion of prostitution
- Money laundering
- Aggravated perjury
- Engaging in organized criminal activity

The following testimony shows how Mike and his lawyer responded to my questions:

Q. (BY MS. CLACK) Okay. Mr. XXXXXXXXXXX, you have in front of you Deposition Exhibit Number 7, which you identify as a document that you've seen before. It's also Bates stamp number XXXX of the documents that we've Produced to you and your attorneys. Now, you sign off on this TB. That is Texas Browning; is it not?

A. It was a moniker for, yes.

Q. So when you're using the name Texas Browning, you sometimes use TB; is that correct?

A. I used to.

Q. But during the time frame that you were doing it and certainly at the time that you sent this E-mail to Jeanne Jones on March 1st, 2012, you were using the name Texas Browning?

A. It was a mistake.

Q. Well, listen to my question, sir. You were using the name Texas Browning on another website; is that correct?

MR. LINDEMOOD: And I'm going to instruct my client to assert the Fifth Amendment privilege, and I'm going to tell you not to answer the question.

Q. Is that what your answer is, that you're going to take the Fifth Amendment?

A. At my attorney's directions, yeah.

Q. Okay. So when you, sir, swore under oath in front of Judge Rucker that you didn't know who Texas Browning was, you were not being truthful to Judge Rucker, were you, sir?

MR. LINDEMOOD: Again, I'm going to instruct my client to assert the Fifth Amendment privilege and direct you not to answer the question.

Q. Is that your answer, sir, that you're going to take the Fifth Amendment?

A. At my attorney's directions.

Q. Okay. Sir, you testified under oath that you had been with several prostitutes over the years. That was true, was it not?

A. I'm going to plead the Fifth Amendment on that.

Q. Sir, you've already testified that you did. Are you saying that that was true testimony, or was that not true when you told Judge Rucker that you had been with prostitutes?

A. I'm going to plead the Fifth Amendment on that.

Q. But it is your testimony that you accidently used the name—or the sign-off letters TB when you were talking to Jeanne Jones?

A. That's correct.

Q. Does your mother, XXXXXXXXXXXXX, know that you have been involved with prostitutes during your marriage?

MR. LINDEMOOD: Objection. Form.

A. Yes.

Q. Does she know the extent and the number of prostitutes that you have been involved with?

MR. LINDEMOOD: Objection. Form.

A. My wife told her a lot.

Q. Okay. So is the answer yes, that she knows that you've been involved with over 90 prostitutes during your marriage?

MR. LINDEMOOD: I'm going to instruct my client to assert the Fifth Amendment privilege and to not answer that question.

Q. I'm asking what your mother knows. Does your mother know or believe that you have been with over 90 prostitutes during the marriage?

A. My mother knows that I have had some indiscretions.

Q. Okay. With prostitutes?

A. My wife made sure she told that.

Q. With prostitutes?

A. That's what my wife told her.

Q. Okay. And that is true that you have had what you call indiscretions with prostitutes; is that right?

A. That's what my wife told her.

Q. Did you admit to your mother that it was true?

A. We've had several discussions about it.

Q. Sir, my question is, did you admit to your mother that it was true?

MR. LINDEMOOD: Again, I'm going to instruct my client to assert the Fifth Amendment privilege and to not answer the question.

Q. Sir, is that what you're choosing to do, that you're going to take the Fifth?

A. At my attorney's directions.

Q. Okay. You are aware that based upon your wife's sworn testimony that—you were not present during her deposition last week, but you are aware, are you not, sir, that documents have been turned over to the Midland Police Department?

A. That's what I've been told.

Q. Okay. And you know that from her sworn testimony? She swore to it.

A. That's what I've been told.

Q. And you also know that the FBI approached her and wanted certain things from her in connection with this case and your activities? Are you aware of that as well?

A. That's what I've been told.

Q. All right. Have you been contacted by the police?

A. No.

Q. Have you been contacted by the FBI?

A. No.

Q. Have you been contacted by any—any type of investigator in connection with criminal activity or allegations of criminal activity on your part?

A. No.

Q. Okay. And, sir, do you know that prostitution is illegal—

A. That's what I've been told.

Q. —in this state? It's what you've been told? Is that what you answer was?

A. Yes.

Q. Okay. Well, do you believe it to be true that it is—prostitution is illegal in the state of Texas?

A. That's what I've been told.

Q. Well, my question was, do you believe that to be a fact that it is illegal in the state of Texas?

A. That's what I've been told.

Q. So is that, yes, you believe that's true?

A. Yes.

Q. Okay. And do you believe that promotion of prostitution is illegal?

A. I'm not sure.

Q. You don't know whether promotion of prostitution is illegal?

A. What is promotion?

Q. What would your understanding of promoting prostitution be?

A. I'm asking you, ma'am.

MR. LINDEMOOD: Objection. Form.

Q. No, sir. I'm asking you. What is your understanding of what promotion of prostitution—

A. I'm asking you what your definitive question is ma'am.

Q. Okay. You don't have a concept of what promotion of prostitution is?

A. I'm wanting to make sure I understand your question, ma'am.

Q. Well sir, if you don't know what promotion of prostitution is at the age of 60 after you have admitted that you've been involved with prostitutes, I'll leave that answer alone, but

I will give you the opportunity one more time. Do you believe that promotion—or understand that promotion of prostitution is a crime in the state of Texas?

A. What is promotion, ma'am? I'm asking you.

Q. You don't know is your answer?

A. I want to make sure I know.

Q. Okay. Well, you want to talk to your attorney about it? We can go off the record. Would you like to talk to your attorney? Let's just do that.

MR. LINDEMOOD: No. There's no reason to go off.

Q. Do you want to talk to your attorney about the term promotion of prostitution?

A. I'm asking you, ma'am, what is your—

Q. I'll move on. Do you know what organized crime is?

A. I've never been involved in it.

Q. Oh, I don't know that you have or haven't, sir. Do you know what it is?

A. What you read in the newspapers, what you read on TV?

Q. What do you read and understand to be organized crime?

A. Only what I see in the newspaper, what you read on TV. Never been around organized crime.
(Exhibits XXXXXXXXXXX marked)

Q. Let's look at the Texas Penal Code Section 71.02, engaging in organized criminal activity. Let me just hand you a copy of it. And I don't have an extra copy, but we can go off the record for a moment and let you and your attorney look at it together if you'd like to look at it. But I'm going to hand you a copy of the printout of the Texas Penal Code. So just—we'll stop the recording and give you a chance to look at it, okay?

Q. (BY MS. CLACK) Sir, we've been off the record for ten minutes. Mr. XXXXXXXXXXXX, we've been off the record for ten minutes, and you've had a chance to look at what I've marked as Deposition Exhibits XXXXXXXXX and XX, have you not?

A. I glanced at it, yes, ma'am.

Q. And the one I've marked as Deposition Exhibit Number X I have highlighted is the definitions from the Texas Penal Code 43.02, the definition of prostitution, and Penal Code 43.03, promotion of prostitution. Have you had a chance to look at those definitions from the Texas Penal Code?

A. I will.

Q. Well, we'll go off the record again while you read those definitions.

Q. (BY MS. CLACK) Sir, let me hand you what's been marked as Deposition Exhibit Number X which we were talking about right before we took a break to give you time to read the two sections of the penal code that deal with prostitution and promotion of prostitution. Did you have a chance to read through those sections of the penal code?

A. I will read them now.

Q. No, sir, did you have a chance during our break to read them?

A. I read your highlighted marks as you instructed me to.

Q. Sir, let me ask you. In reading Deposition Exhibit X—I believe you've already testified under oath that you have participated in being involved with prostitutes. You testified to that on July 11th, 2012; is that correct? Is that how you testified in front of Judge Rucker at the hearing?

MR. LINDEMOOD: I will instruct my client to assert the Fifth Amendment privilege not to answer the question. The testimony will speak for itself.

Q. Is that what you're going to say, that you're not—you're going to take the Fifth Amendment as to your involvement with prostitution?

A. I'm going to do as my attorney advises.

Q. Which is what?

A. To assert the Fifth Amendment.

Q. Okay. Now let's look at the next section that's highlighted on Deposition X, the promotion of prostitution. You were asking me earlier to define it. You've now had a chance to look at it with the Texas Penal Code.

A. I'll read it at this time.

Q. Okay. Okay. Sir, have you been involved with the promotion of prostitution as defined by the Texas Penal Code Section 43.03?

MR. LINDEMOOD: I'm going to instruct my client to assert the Fifth Amendment privilege and to not answer the question.

Q. Is that what you choose to do, sir?

A. At the instructions of my attorney.

Q. Okay. Now let's look at Deposition Exhibit Number X, which is Texas Penal Code Section 34.02, money laundering. Have you had a chance to look at that definition of section 34.02 of the Texas Penal Code on money laundering?

A. Okay.

Q. Okay. Sir, have you been involved in money laundering as defined by Section 34.02 of the Texas Penal Code?

MR. LINDEMOOD: And I'm going to instruct my client to assert the Fifth Amendment privilege and instruct you to not answer the question.

Q. Sir, is that your answer, that you're refusing to answer based upon the Fifth Amendment not to incriminate yourself that you've been involved in money laundering?

A. At the directions of my attorney.

Q. Now let me show you Deposition Exhibit Number XX, which is section—Texas Penal Code Section 37.03, aggravated perjury. Take a moment and look at the definition of aggravated perjury as it says is a third-degree felony when you make a false statement during or in connection with an official proceeding. Okay. You see that definition of aggravated perjury?

A. I read it.

Q. Okay. All right. Sir, have you been involved and committed aggravated perjury as defined by Section 37.03 of the Texas Penal Code?

MR. LINDEMOOD: I'm going to instruct my client to assert his Fifth Amendment privilege and instruct him not to answer the question.

Q. Sir, is that what you are choosing to do is to refuse to answer the questions about your involvement with aggravated perjury?

A. At the advice of my attorney.

Q. Thank you. Now let's look at Deposition Exhibit Number XX, which is Texas Penal Code Section 71.02, engaging in organized criminal activity. Where a person commits an offense with the intent to establish, maintain, or participate in the combination of the profits or as a member of a criminal street gang he commits to conspire one or more of the following: The promotion of prostitution and aggravated promotion of prostitution.

Sir, I'm going to ask you based upon the definition of the Texas Penal Code of engaging in organized criminal activity whether you have participated in organized criminal activity?

MR. LINDEMOOD: I'm going to instruct my client to assert the Fifth Amendment privilege, and I'm going to instruct him also to not answer the question.

Q. Sir, is that your answer, that you're going to take the Fifth and refuse to answer the question?

A. At the advice of my attorney.

From the time I was hired by Karen in June 2012, we worked on multiple matters in connection with her divorce. In doing so, we accumulated a large amount of documentation regarding Mike's activities with sex trafficking. As of this writing, I have not heard anything from law enforcement regarding the investigation or prosecution of this sex trafficking scheme operating in Midland, Texas.

The Texas prostitution law has changed since this case of 2012. Effective September 1, 2021, it is now a felony for a person who commits an offense if the person knowingly offers or agrees to receive a fee from another to engage in sexual conduct (Texas Penal Code 43:02 Prostitution). The State of Texas is the first state to make buying sex a felony.

PUZZLE PIECES

- Do you see evidence of organized crime in this case?
- Do you have questions regarding the number of people participating in and aiding the Providers and Hobbyists?
- Do you have questions regarding law enforcement (the FBI and Midland Police) and their failure to follow up on the evidence turned over to them?
- Do you have questions about following the money paid to the Provider and the hotel?
- Why were these expensive suites easily and regularly available to the sex workers in a town where hotels were otherwise regularly full?

- Were the names chosen by the moderators ("Antichrist 666" and "Cryptkicker") significant to identify what organized crime group was running this operation?
- Who and what organization were behind the ECCIE website?
- Were the men who participated with these Providers now subject to being controlled and blackmailed by some organized crime group?
- Why were men from Las Vegas showing up with the county judge at Mike's house looking at his gun collection and the room where he kept his Hobby phone?
- Do you think that the young women who were the Providers on the ECCIE website were free to leave or get out any time they wanted?

Chapter 8

TRICKERY AND COLLUSION

"In most states, the first time that the public learns about a state judge's misconduct is when a judicial conduct commission files formal charges."[1]

In 2010, I was hired by the mother in a custody dispute. The case was pending in Midland, Texas. The judge was Dean Rucker. Eventually, I paid the jury fee to request a trial before twelve jurors to decide the ultimate issue of who should be named as sole managing conservator.

The lawyer representing the dad was David McClure, a board-certified family law specialist from El Paso, Texas. David's wife was Justice Ann McClure, a respected justice on the Eighth Court of Appeals in El Paso.

After months of depositions and pretrial discovery, we had a two-week trial before a Midland jury in May 2011. They named my client as the sole managing conservator and said I should be awarded $320,000 in attorney's fees.

The local rules for the Midland Courts required that final orders and judgments shall be submitted to the judge for signature within thirty days after the verdict. In compliance with the local rules, I submitted a proposed judgment in alignment with the jury's findings. Weeks, and then months, went by, and Judge Rucker had not signed my proposed judgment. He did not give me any instruction or direction or hearings to explain what was wrong with it or why he would not sign it.

On October 4, 2011, I received a shocking letter from Judge Rucker completely gutting the jury verdict. I filed an objection to this ruling and instruction. My objection contained a footnote that contained the words *trickery* and *collusion*.

Four days after I filed my objection, Dean Rucker completely withdrew the letter ruling and stated he was going to reconsider his ruling. A month later, Dean Rucker sent a new ruling in alignment with the jury verdict with one exception—he denied making the dad pay my attorney's fees.

Although something in my objection convinced Judge Rucker to reconsider his long letter of gutting the jury verdict, David McClure filed a motion for sanctions against me for using the words *trickery* and *collusion* in the footnote.

The visiting judge who came in to hear the sanctions motion found that I should be sanctioned and ordered me to pay Mr. Wollschlager (the dad) $17,670 for the attorney fees he had incurred in paying McClure for bringing his sanctions motion.

I appealed the sanctions order. The appellate judge who wrote the opinion upholding the sanctions against me was Justice Mike Willson, who had been sworn into that position by Judge Dean Rucker. Willson was from Midland. Justice Willson's first opinion was signed on December 19, 2013.

My appellate lawyers wrote brilliant briefs and did a great job. In fact, they did such a great job that Justice Willson withdrew his

December 19, 2013, opinion and replaced it with another opinion dated May 15, 2014. The second opinion had an entirely different writing style and different reasoning but, nevertheless, left the sanctions order in place.

The following pages are excerpts from the brief filed by my attorneys at the law firm of Beck Redden L.L.P. on January 17, 2013. It is on file in the official records of the Court of Appeals in Eastland, Texas, No. 11-12-00269-CV, Clack vs. Wollschlager.

Ultimately, I paid over $100,000 in attorney's fees to fight a sanctions order of $17,670. I appealed this order to set out the facts and circumstances that led up to my usage of the words *trickery* and *collusion* in the footnote and for the whole world to know, at least from my perspective, what "justice" looked like in Midland, Texas, when I won a jury trial in May 2011 and how the presiding judge attempted to gut that jury verdict. Consider this just another piece of the larger puzzle of the Midland justice system.

Portions of the brief filed by my attorney for the Court of Appeals in Eastland, Texas, follow:

DINNER NO. 1—AUGUST 2010

A few months after the mother filed this suit, Ms. Clack happened to see the judge and Mr. McClure dining together at conference for family law specialists. RR158-60.* It gave her pause that they would choose to sit next to each other even when Mr. McClure had a "highly contested case" in

----

* The numbers and letters listed in this appeal and those following refer to exhibits and page numbers within the official court record and have been included here for the reader's reference.

the judge's court. RR158-59. Ms. Clack watched the two of them interact and concluded that she owed it to her client to request a trial by jury. *Id.* "I wanted to take the pressure off of the judge and allow the jury to make the decisions." RR159. While the case had been on the bench trial docket for months, she paid the fee and requested a jury trial shortly thereafter. CRl:133.

THE JURY TRIAL

During the two-week trial, Mr. McClure exhibited familiarity with the court's staff and office space in a way that caught the attention of the mother's trial team. He was seen coming from the hallway by the judge's private chambers several times. RR39-41, 126-127, 143-46, 165, 182-184. And when the judge instructed Ms. Clack's employee to ask his court administrator to email a subpoenaed document, the court administrator responded that she could not because she was working on . . . Mr. McClure's personal request, Mr. McClure stood behind the court administrator's desk in the hall by the judge's office. PX5.

By contrast, the mother's trial team used the court's public areas for making copies or getting coffee. RR145. "That familiarity of going back into the hallway and getting coffee, we weren't doing anything like that during this trial." RR145-46. They were sensitive to the fact that Mr. McClure was not making the same choices.

DINNER NO. 2—AUGUST 2011

While Ms. Clack was dining at a restaurant on the San Antonio Riverwalk, she was quite surprised to see the judge and Mr. McClure walk in together with a small group of 7 or 8. This occasion was a private dinner with reservations—not in the seminar setting where judges and attorneys commonly dine together. RR131. They were seated at the table next to Ms. Clack. RR131. Just as they had earlier in the life of this case, Mr. McClure and the judge sat right next to each other. CR3:897. Ms. Clack was "shocked." RR131. But she had already won the verdict, and she tried to reassure herself that her client had nothing to worry about. RR 131.

The brief went on to state:

THE OCTOBER 4TH LETTER RULING

The trial court set forth all its rulings in a 12-page letter. CR2:351-63. The letter recited that "the Court may not contravene a jury verdict on the issue of the appointment of a sole managing conservator." CR2:351. But then it proceeded to restrict the mother's exclusive rights. CR2:352-58. The letter ordered where the child would reside (the Court chose Midland County, as the father had requested); ordered which doctor would be the child's primary care physician (the Court chose the father's requested doctor); and ordered that all decisions about the child's education had to be made jointly by the parents (as the father requested).

While the jury found that the mother's reasonable and necessary attorney's fees for trial were $320,000, the letter ordered each party to pay their own fees, expenses, and costs; it then cut the requested child support by half. (CR2:359-61).

Most alarmingly of all, the letter stated that the Court had retained the right to modify the sole managing conservator's exclusive rights because "neither party . . . requested a jury question regarding the imposition of a geographic restriction. Neither did they object to the Court's charge." CR2:356. For reasons Ms. Clack would soon explain, this implication of charge waiver left her blindsided.

Perhaps the only ruling that did not favor the father was the part ordering the father to pay 100% of all healthcare expenses. CR2:360. Mr. Wollschlager's inexplicable generosity of six days earlier was now highly suspicious.

In its concluding paragraph, the letter directed to Ms. Clack to draft orders in accordance with these letter rulings (as if she had prevailed). CR2:362.

THE MOTHER OBJECTS

Ms. Clack instead filed a motion explaining her objections in great detail. CR2:264-497.* This 14-page motion was styled, "Motion for Judgment to Conform With the Jury Verdict." It was supported by a hefty stack of exhibits. In it, she was forced to rehash all the evidence supporting the jury's findings. She emphasized that the Court had improperly weighed

----

* Ms. Clack associated another attorney, Claudia Donaldson, to write the motion. Both of their names appear on the motion, and they stand by their grounds and good faith in all of its contents.

the evidence and had issued rulings that could not be squared with the verdict or the statutes.

The mother objected vigorously to the restrictions on the child's residence. The father had never pleaded for this restriction until the verdict. Likewise, "[t]he Court never made known or even hinted to the mother's lawyer that he would consider a geographic restriction should the jury vote for a *Sole Managing Conservator.*" CR2:368. The Court's charge had been specifically predicated to get jury findings on a geographic restriction if the jury found that the parents should be *Joint Managing Conservators*, and the letter ruling noted that no one had objected to the jury charge. CR2:367-68. This was too much for Ms. Clack, who read the letter to imply that there had been waiver. In her opinion, the ruling could not be explained by the law or the evidence.

The motion dropped a footnote airing a deeper concern: *Further, this rises to the level of trickery on the part of the Court and smacks of collusion between counsel for [the father] and the Court.* CR2:368. The motion's authors could not understand this highly irregular course of events.

THE COURT WITHDRAWS ITS OCTOBER 4TH LETTER RULING

Three days later, the Court sent a new letter. It states in full: The Court is of the opinion this case merits further consideration. The letter ruling of October 4, 2011, is withdrawn. The Court also rescinds its order of November 4, 2011, directing the preparation and submission of the final order in this case. CR2:498 (dated 11/7/11).

THE FATHER MOVES FOR SANCTIONS

Perhaps sensing defeat, the father immediately filed a full-blown merits response and requested sanctions under Rule 13. CR2:504-56. The mother filed a response limited to the motion for sanctions. CR557-62; 3:878-88.

THE COURT AGREES WITH THE MOTHER'S MOTION ON THE MERITS AND REFERS OUT THE MOTION FOR SANCTIONS

In the wake of these motions, the Court issued its final letter. CR2:566-74. Showing great sensitivity to the mother's legal positions, the letter has a very different tone and outcome from the original one. It began by recognizing that "Sole managing conservatorship is not simply a hollow title." CR2:567. It agreed with the mother that the restrictions on her rights appeared contrary to the verdict: "It would seem to contravene a jury verdict naming a person as a sole managing conservator if a trial court imposes limitations on the exclusive rights and duty of a sole managing conservator[.]" CR2:569. It acknowledged that it had not seen any case support for placing restrictions on a sole managing conservator following a jury verdict. CR2:569. It totally changed course on most of its initial rulings:

> Despite its worthy intentions, the Court's initial letter ruling of October 4, 2011, which has since been withdrawn, failed to strike a proper balance between the trial court's power to impose limitations on the exclusive rights and duty of a sole managing conservator and the statutory prohibition against contravening a jury verdict naming a party as a sole managing conservator.

CR2:570. The letter returned to the mother the victory she won with the jury. Her Motion for Judgment to Conform With the Jury Verdict had been validated.

The letter did *not* award the mother her attorney's fees of $320,000. CR2:573. The Court and jury had seen evidence that prior litigation with the father had depleted all the mother's funds, and that the father happened to be a multi-millionaire who could easily bear this expense. CR1:270-75; 2:373-74; 2:438-63. Despite the Court's decision to present the question of attorney's fees to the jury, the Court chose to award no fees, expenses, or even court costs to the mother.

The Court decided the sanctions motion should be sent to a different judge, and it signed an Order for Referral, asking that a different judge be assigned to hear the motion. CR2:563,574. The judge assigned to hear the sanctions motions was the Hon. Les Hatch of the 237th District Court in Lubbock County. CR3:824.

THE SANCTIONS HEARING

Even before the day of the sanctions hearing, it became apparent that the father's team might have lost sight of the issue. For example, to prepare for the hearing, the father's team requested transcripts of testimony from doctors at trial. CR4:909-10. Ms. Clack filed an objection to retrying the lawsuit through the sanctions hearing, and explained the narrow scope of the issue. CR4:909-11.

Mr. McClure also viewed the sanctions hearing as though his integrity were on trial. He wanted to defend himself and the judge. He subpoenaed Judge Rucker to testify and pushed hard on this point: "It's an allegation that's been made, Judge. And I have to defend Judge Rucker, and I have to defend myself. And [Judge Rucker] needs to take the stand. . . . I want to ask him questions: Did you engage in some type of trickery in this charge? Did you collude with me?" RR12. Mr. McClure had evidently lost sight of the precise issue under Rule 13, and he treated this hearing as a platform to disprove the footnote.

A lawyer from the state appeared on Judge Rucker's behalf and fought equally hard against having the judge testify:

"This is the first time that I've ever had a situation where the party alleging that the judge did nothing wrong is the one seeking to subpoena him. Normally it's the other way around."

"But it's my understanding that Ms. Clack has no real objection to my motion [to quash], and my only real problem is Mr. McClure."

RR10-11. The judge ultimately sustained the motion to quash. RR234.

Since Mr. Wollschlager was the sanctions movant, he had the burden of proof and went first. He first called the mother's attorneys, Ms. Donaldson and Ms. Clack. They testified to the evidence already discussed in this Statement of Facts. RR17-177; 118-70. And they both stood by their belief that they had facts giving rise to the concern expressed in the footnote. In fact, Ms. Clack testified that she had consulted a variety of experienced judges and lawyers. The consensus view was that the judge's ruling was "shocking":

[W]hen Ms. Donaldson came in as an outsider, someone who's not daily in the practice of family law, but very knowledgeable, I was shocked, and she was shocked. We even consulted with other lawyers. We consulted with—with lawyers out of Amarillo. We consulted with other lawyers around the state, consulted with retired judges. . . . I consulted with Sally Emerson of Amarillo, her husband, Judge Emerson of Amarillo, the district judge there. I consulted with College professors down in Houston. I consulted with my own parents, retired judges themselves, and as I said, my stepmother is a retired district and Supreme Court justice. I consulted with retired justices locally. The consensus was that this ruling was shocking, shocking. RR132-34.

Mr. Wollschlager then testified very briefly. RR171-75. Finally, Mr. McClure testified, denying that anything improper had happened between himself and the judge. RR176-214. They were afforded an opportunity to offer their own explanations for the various facts relied on by the mother. For example, Mr. Wollschlager testified about the reason he suddenly paid 100% of his son's orthotics: "It was generosity. Nothing more." RR173.

Mr. McClure testified that he billed more than <u>60 hours</u> pursuing sanctions for the footnote. RR198. He had traveled back and forth to Midland from El Paso reviewed testimony, wrote the sanctions motion and prepared for trial. *Id.* He also had his paralegals spend <u>38 hours</u> building their attack on the footnote. RR198-99. He asked the judge to award their hourly rates for all of this as sanctions against the mother's attorneys: "My client should not have to be paying for this." RR198.

The mother's side went next, first calling the author of the ominous text message, Nancy Jones. RR214-30. Ms. Jones was Larry Wollschlager's former office manager and was friends with Kimberly Carlson (the mother). RR106. She had sent the mother's team text messages and met with them to discuss her "personal knowledge and interactions between McClure, Wollschlager, and supposedly with Judge Rucker." RR106-07. Ms. Clack immediately asker her:

Q. How did you have information on September 29th about the basis of what's said in that text message?

Ms. Jones testified: "I had people talk to me and tell me some things that were going on." RR215. Before Ms. Clack could ask the next question, Mr. McClure jumped up to object to hearsay (even though the truth or falsity of the text message was not an issue). *Id.* The lawyer who was at the hearing to represent Judge Rucker also jumped up to object, insisting she lacked personal knowledge. *Id.* The two of them successfully cut off this line of questioning, and Ms. Clack moved on. "Okay. I'll just move on because the text speaks for itself." RR216.

Ms. Jones also testified about Mr. McClure's statements to her. He had said right before the jury trial that the case was a "slam dunk because we had the case in the bag." RR216. He had mentioned that he was friends with the judge. RR217. He even told her about his family connection with the judge: Judge Rucker's father (a lawyer) had represented his father (also a lawyer). RR229.

Ms. Jones was not merely a passive observer of this lawsuit; she had served as a witness for the father's side and had helped prepare for the trial. RR147,227. None of this was disputed. Mr. McClure even elicited the testimony that they had talked "quite a bit about the evidence in this case." RR218.

The mother's side also called the mother, Kimberly Carlson, to testify about the episode where Mr. Wollschlager paid 100% of his son's medical expenses 6 days before the ruling came out ordering him to do so. RR230-31. She emphasized how unusual this was; he had never once paid for more than his half of any expenses before. RR231.

The presiding judge, the Hon. Les Hatch, later issued a letter ruling concluding that Rule 13 had been violated. CR4:931-32. The letter requested that Mr. McClure prepare the order.

THE SANCTIONS ORDER

The sanctions order is expressly based on Rule 13. Tab C; CR4:96. It awards Mr. Wollschlager sanctions against both of the mother's attorneys for $17,670.[1] The order finds that the footnote was groundless and made in bad faith, but it does not find that the footnote was brought for purposes of harassment (which is an alternative ground for sanctions under Rule 13).

The order is 7 pages, making detailed findings of good cause that thoroughly address Mr. McClure's side of the evidence. But it does not acknowledge all the facts available to the mother's team at the time the footnote was written. For example, the order forgets to mention that the mother was sent a text message warning of the judge's adverse ruling—just five days before the ruling arrived.

In addition to the actions described above, the brief filed by my appellate attorney went on to point out the following:

The movant failed to prove that the footnote was groundless. The relevant question is whether the movant proved that Ms. Clack had no factual or legal grounds, on November 4, 2011, that supported the footnote.

Five days before the Court issued its ruling. Ms. Carlson (the mother) received an ominous text message:

We will see next week when rucker rules. He and mcclure r up to something. U r still the better parent, U hv been and will be. PX12; RR104-07, 142-43, 147-48, 215.

Just as predicted, the judge ruled the following week. CR2:351; RR137-38.

Of course, if the judge's ruling had conformed to the jury's verdict, this array of facts, culminating in the text message, would have been dismissed as nothing. But the ruling turned each star into a seemingly connected constellation.

"[I]t was incredibly beyond coincidence that David McClure would 11 days after having a private dinner with the judge be filing this motion for a geographic restriction." RR132. When the judge actually entertained this post-verdict request and implied in its letter that she had waived objections to it by not objecting to the jury charge, she was stunned. "And the combination of all these things was so shocking." RR132.

Without the text message and the father's unprecedented decision to pay for 100% of his son's medical expenses, these facts admittedly would not be enough to overcome the benefit of the doubt. But close social contact with a judge during a pending case, lingering in the court's private office space, and asking favors of court personnel can be interpreted as suggesting a high level of familiarity. Ms. Clack

> also testified that she found it very disturbing that Mr. McClure would comment to her "that [he] felt that Judge Rucker would come in and take care of [him] even—even after the jury trial[.]" RR169-70.
>
> I mean, his alliance with Rucker and his confidence that Rucker was going to rule favorably for him was just over and over and over again. I mean, throughout the two years that I have been the lawyer representing Kim Carlson, Mr. McClure has regularly treated this with quite confidence that Rucker will rule in his favor. That gives me great concern. That is against our Texas lawyers creed. We are not to be representing that we have special favor with the Court. We're not to imply it. And it has regularly been over and over again indicated in this case.

The brief quoted the statements I made in court from the sanctions hearing:

> "And when I combined that with that text message from Nancy Jones and what she will be testifying to later in this hearing, it is—they knew something was going on that we didn't know on our side. It was some extrajudicial conduct and certainly evidence that there was communication going on."

PUZZLE PIECES

- What does this case tell you about justice in this particular county and what happens even when the lawyer plays by the rules?

- What does this case and the appellant brief tell you about going against a multimillionaire client when his lawyer has a certain history with the judge?
- What does this case tell you about methods to discourage lawyers and clients who point out appearances of favor or ex parte communication for one side?
- What does this case tell you about justice in Midland County, Texas, during the years of 2011 and 2012?
- Do you believe other lawyers and clients who hear about this case and this kind of treatment toward the "winning" lawyer and client are discouraged to take on hard cases and wealthy parties on the other side?
- Do you see how some lawyers would give up trying because of this type of treatment and conduct or just join the Club?

Chapter 9

ON THE PAYROLL

For two decades, Petty managed a covert balancing act: He was both prosecutor and de facto judge, pocketing an extra $250,000 for his dishonest services.[1]

In a small notice in the June 2021 issue of the *Texas Bar Journal*, the following matter was reported:

> "On April 13, 2021, the Supreme Court of Texas accepted the resignation, in lieu of discipline of WELDON RALPH PETTY JR. [#15866500], of Midland. At the time of his resignation, Petty had three grievances pending alleging Petty represented opposing parties in the same related matter. Petty violated Rule 1.06(b)(2)."[2]

Ralph Petty had served as an assistant district attorney in Midland for many years. I thought of him as a good appellate lawyer in criminal cases. The only real contact I had with him was that he placed his name in consideration for judge of the 109th Judicial District Court (Andrews, Winkler, and Crane Counties). My dad had retired from that position, creating a vacancy, which the governor of Texas was tasked with filling. Although Petty wanted the job, he did not receive the appointment; however, he continued to work as an assistant district attorney in Midland, Texas.

During the winter of 2020 and 2021, Petty's name came up in connection to a disturbing story that stated that Ralph was working for and getting paid by the district judges in Midland while he was working at the same time as assistant district attorney. He was their briefing clerk and paid thousands of dollars over a period of many years. The reports from various sources on the internet said this went on for twenty years, and Petty had been paid around $250,000 during this period for his services for the judges. All of this was going on while Petty was also serving as a prosecutor in the Midland district attorney's office on the same cases.

One of the cases on which Petty worked for both the district attorney as a prosecutor and for the district judge as a briefing clerk was a 2003 capital murder case in which the defendant Clint Young received the death penalty. Young had been on death row awaiting execution for years.

After the news became public about Petty's double role in that trial, Mr. Young's attorneys succeeded in overturning their client's conviction and death sentence, granting him a new trial. The judge who had presided over the capital murder trial of Mr. Young was John Hyde, now deceased.

The story of the unethical conduct by Petty, who retired in 2019; the Midland district attorneys (Al Schorre and Teresa Clingman); and the Midland district judges is reported and discussed in multiple publications and sites. The articles I consulted point out various highlights: three hundred criminal defendants, $250,000, twenty years.

As I searched the internet, I found articles and references to this story in multiple places, including the following:

- *USA Today*, February 4, 2021[3]
- *Wall Street Journal*, April 11, 2022[4]
- Institute for Justice, April 11, 2022; Erma Wilson filed a federal lawsuit with attorneys Robert McNamara and Jaba Tsitsuashvili[5]
- *Texas Observer*, September 19, 2023 (in partnership with the Garrison Project)[6]
- *Midland Reporter Telegram*, April 12, 2022[7]
- NewsWest9, September 20, 2023[8]
- *Ethics Alarms*, May 17, 2021, by Jack Marshall[9]

One of the people who wrote about the story of Petty and the Midland District Judges was Jack Marshall.* I found Jack Marshall's article to be insightful in that he is a lawyer and an expert on ethics. Here is what Mr. Marshall wrote:

----

* Jack Marshall, the primary writer of *Ethics Alarms*, is president and founder of ProEthics (http://www.proethics.com). He has taken the experience gleaned from a diverse career in law, public policy, academia, and theater and applied it to the field of legal, business, workplace, and organizational ethics. A graduate of Harvard College, where he specialized in American government and leadership, and Georgetown University Law Center, he practiced criminal law in Massachusetts and organizational law in the District of Columbia and led nonprofit organizations devoted to education, public policy research, and health.

A SCANDAL THAT COMPELS THE QUESTION: IF THIS CAN HAPPEN, WHAT OTHER ETHICS ROT LURKS IN THE JUSTICE SYSTEM?

MAY 17, 2021/JACK MARSHALL

Texas attorney Weldon Ralph Petty Jr. was a busy guy at the Midland County courthouse. By day he appeared before judges as an associate District attorney. By night, he worked as a law clerk for some of the same judges, sometimes advising them regarding the criminal cases he was prosecuting. This went on for more than a decade.

You don't have to be a legal ethics whiz to figure out that such conduct isn't ethical. Prosecutors are barred from privately communicating with judges about cases or matters even indirectly related to their cases. Judges and their clerks are forbidden from disclosing the discussions and in chambers considerations regarding cases to prosecutors or defense attorneys.

Thus Petty, 78, was flagrantly violating ethics rules by simultaneously acting as a prosecutor and a paid advisor to supposedly impartial judges, who were also breaching judicial ethics to a spectacular degree by allowing him to do so. A February story published by *USA Today* first reported that Petty was paid by judges as a clerk in a least 350 cases from 2001 until his retirement as an assistant disctrict attorney in mid-2019. Seventy-three defendants, maybe more, that Petty prosecuted are in prison. A court opinion issued April 28 calls for overturning Midland County's only death penalty case due to Petty's prosecutorial misconduct and the judge's failure to recuse himself, so Clinton Lee Young, who has been on death row since Petty prosecuted him in 2003, will get a new trial.

Petty surrendered his law license to avoid being disbarred—you know, like Bill Clinton did in Arkansas—and is likely to avoid any other sanctions. This is Texas, after all; formal disciplinary action against a current or former prosecutor is rare everywhere, and it is extremely rare in the Lone Star State.

In his opinion regarding Young's case, Judge Sid Harle described Petty's behavior as "shocking prosecutorial misconduct that destroyed any semblance of a fair trial." Harle found that Petty violated Young's due process rights, and that Judge John Hyde, who employed Petty while he presided over the trial, should have disqualified himself from the case. Harle has recommended that all judgments entered against Young to be declared "null and void."

Petty's conflicts of interest as well as the dual state paychecks he received for continuing them were allowed to continue under two previous elected district attorneys in Midland, who also failed to disclose his conflicts to defendants and their attorneys, including Young's lawyers. Petty's contract in 2001 allowed moonlighting, which would have been permissible if the moonlighting didn't involve the cases he was prosecuting or judges he was appearing in front of in court. The district attorneys did nothing to stop Petty's misconduct even after his paychecks from the prosecution and from the judiciary were questioned by the Internal Revenue Service in a 2008 audit.

Finally, the current Midland County District Attorney, Laura Nodolf, discovered Petty's moonlighting in August of 2019 and disclosed it.

The judge who presided over Young's trial is now dead, but some of the other judges who assisted Petty in his ethics breach are stll alive and on the bench. All of them were complicit in denying defendants their constitutional rights to a fair trial. It remains to be seen if they will be sanctioned. Even if they are, the fact that something like this could happen at all, and for so many years, should have ethics alarms sounding throughout the justice system, and not only in Texas.[10]

These actions and activities are discussed in articles, lawsuits, opinion pieces, and blogs in the referenced publications and lawsuits. They report that Mr. Petty was paid around $250,000 over a couple of decades. This clearly unethical conduct by someone in the district attorney's office and the Midland district judges affected the lives of many people going through the judicial system in Midland, Texas. Although Mr. Petty turned in his law license in 2021 and is not able to practice law again, there is no public record or information that any action has been taken against the Midland judges who participated in this scheme.

PUZZLE PIECES

- As you add this puzzle piece of information to the growing pattern of judicial conduct in Midland County, Texas, do you question the presence of systemic abuse?

- Do you question whether there was abuse not only toward the people who were prosecuted but possible favor toward decisions being made not to prosecute certain individuals?
- Do you question why nothing changes in this arrangement after 2008 when the Internal Revenue Service revealed that Ralph Petty was on the payroll?
- What attitudes, arrogance, and arrangements allowed this conduct to go on for so long?
- Why is there no action revealed regarding the judges and others who participated and/or looked the other way in this scheme?

Chapter 10

SOMETHING ABOUT MARY

Approximately one in four children experiences child abuse or neglect in their lifetime.[1]

On June 5, 2013, I began representing a client named Mary. She had a son who was seven years old, and there had been some form of open litigation going on with her ex-husband for years. She and her son's father were fairly regularly filing motions and going to court over geographic restrictions, parental rights, payment of child support and medical bills, educational decisions, and so forth.

Mary did not trust her ex-husband's decisions on parenting and co-parenting, so she had a need to keep a lawyer on retainer, just in case. Before we met, her lawyer was David Lindemood. She was satisfied that he had done a proper job representing her in her efforts to keep her son safe, but Lindemood had been elected to be the next judge for the 318th Judicial District Court, as Dean Rucker was retiring and taking senior status. Dean Rucker was becoming the administrative judge for the 7th Region covering thirty-eight counties. When Lindemood became the district judge, he would no longer be able to represent Mary.

The legal skirmishes we dealt with involved concerns that Mary's ex-husband had prepared a bunker on some property near Waco, Texas, which he called Location X. This man and his father were prepared to go there in case he thought he needed to hide out from any attackers or invaders. He carried an EpiPen just in case he was bitten by a zombie.

I quickly understood that Mary and her ex-husband had different philosophies of parenting and child-rearing. She wanted to send their son to the Montessori school, and her ex wanted to hide out at Location X and have weapons such as AK-47s and AR-15s, which he photographed and sent to Mary in text messages.

I spent many hours meeting with Mary and getting to know her background and the details that were significant to the prior legal battles, as well as the potential future battles we would face. It is important for me to be aware of the weaknesses and family history or events that the opposing side might use against my client and their family when we are in court. Getting blindsided in court in the middle of a hearing can be devasting to the outcome of a case.

Here is an example of my questioning: "I need to know about you and your family. Is there anything about you or your family that the other side might bring up that would be embarrassing or harmful to your credibility or reputation?"

Her answer was something like, "Well, yes, from the time I was born until I was ten, my family was caught up and involved with a nondenominational church in Midland that was practicing satanic rituals. It was a satanic cult, but my mom figured it out and helped us get away from the cult."

I said something like, "Oh, okay. Does your ex-husband know this?"

"Yes."

Next, I asked, "Does David Lindemood know this?"

"Yes."

Thus began the long talks I had with Mary about her shocking revelation about her family. Mary's father was a highly placed financial advisor in a well-respected financial institution in Midland. These were not ignorant, backward people.

I had thousands of questions for Mary. How did this happen? How could this happen? Why did this happen? What did you go through as a child? How did it affect you then? How does it affect you today? Do you experience triggers and posttraumatic stress disorder? Do you remember who the people were in the cult? Do you run into them? What do you do now when you encounter them? Why did your parents not figure things out sooner and get you and your siblings out?

This beautiful, brilliant, protective mother had gone through horrific abuse during the first ten years of her life. When her parents got the family away from the cult, Mary had to undergo ten corrective surgeries over the next ten years to repair the damage the cult members had inflicted upon her body.

She described to me how she and her family members were picked up on certain dates (when rituals were taking place), then blindfolded, drugged, and put through multiple events of mental, emotional, and physical torture.

Mary still carries a scar on her forehead between her eyebrows where something punctured her head. She told me she had a brain scan that confirmed some object had penetrated her skull. To me, the size of the scar looked like it could have been caused by an ice pick.

An important aspect about Mary's story is that it seemed to be a different group of people from the ones I described earlier in this book, although both groups were conducting their rituals and practices in Midland, Texas. I learned many things from Mary by listening to her stories and her answering my questions as best she could.

I admire Mary for her courage in sharing these deep, dark secrets from her family history and experience. I also appreciate her willingness to allow me to share her story and her truth in order to help others learn about them and understand that these activities continue to occur. Good people and good families can get caught up in an awful cult, but they can get out, just like Mary's family did.

I told Mary I was including a chapter in this book about her and her family's experience about the satanic cult. I asked her to write what she would like to say to the readers of this book, which I am including below.

> First, I want to thank Cynthia. It was amazing to have a lawyer who understood the history of my personal experience and what my family went through. Ritual abuse is so much more common than anyone wants to admit or see. Often, people don't know what to do with it. At first, neither did Cynthia, but she knew what not to do. She knew not to look the other way or dismiss it. She knew not to hide from it. She knew what most people know when horrible things confront them: that someone needed to act. But here, she separated from the others by actually acting. Cynthia is a woman of action.
>
> In my opinion, people are asking the wrong questions. The most common questions I've heard over the years regarding my story follow the pattern of, "Why did they do that?" "How

did it go on for so long?" "Why didn't your family leave?" "Who knew?"

While it's natural to have these questions and to want to know more, survivors are rarely able to fully answer them. When you've heard these questions enough times, however, it feels natural to attempt to do so, because otherwise, who will believe you? So many victims try to fill in background information that they may not have access to. For example, I don't know what my abusers were thinking when they did the things they did. I was never able to ask them if they worshipped Satan, if they believed in Jesus, if they studied the Bible, or if they wanted me to hate God. As a result, I can only make educated guesses about their reasoning.

When you're born into abuse, you have no way of knowing that what's happening to you isn't normal. It's your normal. It's the only experience you've had. Many people wonder why victims don't leave sooner or why they go back to their abuser. Most of the time, from my experience, it's a conditioned comfort. If you were born in a hole, you would spend most of your pivotal years believing that the hole is all that exists. Why would you imagine anything else?

Try to imagine a color that doesn't exist or a place that you've never seen. The ancient Greeks were brilliant, but they still believed that the stars were speckles of milk in the sky. What else would they be? No one explained to them that there were gigantic balls of gas millions and billions of miles away, just floating around in the void. Why would they think that? For that matter, why would they think that the stars were part of more than Earth's sky?

For that matter, why would a victim of childhood abuse run to a neighbor's house with no way of knowing that it could be better? Revisiting the hole analogy, why would they ask for a ladder if they thought there was nothing besides the hole? Would they even know what a ladder was?

Most seasoned abusers understand this concept. They also understand that the younger the child is, the more the abuse will affect them because of the way the young brain works. Most children can't distinguish fantasy from reality or form a coherent memory until they're about four years old.

Think of the last time you were really upset in a heated argument with another person and how both of you ended up with different ideas of what happened, what was said, and what was meant. Can you explain why they said the things they said? Why didn't you leave as soon as it became tense? If other people were there, did they leave? Why or why not?

Unless the experience you are thinking of was recent and you talked to the other person and everyone else who was there after the argument, there's a good chance that you can't answer all of these questions. Now imagine if you went through an even more emotional experience many years ago, before your memory was fully developed. You would likely find answering those questions impossible, as do many victims of abuse.

Hopefully, I did something just by asking these questions. Hopefully, you see from this point that we are all just humans. As I heard in the rooms, there is a little bit of good in the worst of us and a little bit of bad in the best of us. I also implore you to remember that many abusers are former victims of abuse themselves.

But no matter how hard I've tried to come up with the answers, I know one thing for a fact. I survived. My family survived. Our household had three girls, each five years apart, and two parents. All five of us are alive and well today. After many years of therapy and recovery, I have been able to explain many of the events that occurred in a coherent way, though as a child I could not because I was disassociating during the abuse and threatened with the killings of animals or people who I cared about if I told anyone.

When I was born, these things were already happening, and by the time I was two, we'd moved to Colorado with the entire group because that's just what weird people did, and then they had the great idea that my parents should let a twenty-two-year-old man, and an alcoholic at that, live in our basement. He lived there for two years and sexually abused me along with my seven-year-old sister. Picture a two-year-old—yes, a two-year-old—turning around in the middle of the night and asking the grown man behind her, "Wait a minute. Why are you doing this to me?"

Obviously, that's not what I did. I was too busy pretending to be asleep. During the day, he played games with us and was very fun to be around, which set a precedent for duplicity in myself that took me decades to navigate, a process that was finished only when I faced my own alcoholism. The pattern of enjoying a person in the day and hating them at night set me up for several failed marriages and many toxic relationships with partners.

At one point, my family lived on the same block as our pastor and his family, right next to the church building in which the entire group gathered three times a week or more. We also gathered at the pastor's house twice a week. I believe it is common for cults to isolate their members by keeping them busy so they have no time for anything else, and to keep them close together so they are easier to keep track of and control.

We were also discouraged from seeking professional help of any kind, including doctors when we were sick. The younger two of us three girls were born by midwife at home. We also attended private schools and were homeschooled. My parents were kept busy to the extent that they had no idea what was happening to us children. My mom was abused as well and electrocuted frequently.

The other important thing I would like to point out is that these people have lives of their own. They don't have all day to abuse children. They have jobs, bills to pay, and groceries to buy. They weren't a strictly organized, self-sufficient group like one might imagine. Most of our abuse was on holidays, weekends, and nights—not because they followed some ritualistic calendar but because these were the times they all had off from work. These were ordinary people. The two-year trip to Colorado, however, seemed to plug the cult into a larger group that was more sophisticated.

Our involvement in the group came to a turning point when my older sister found herself too weak to pull her shriveled sixty-nine-pound body out of the bathtub at the age of sixteen. She was admitted to a hospital in Dallas, tube-fed, and given twenty-four-hour supervision. It was here that she told doctors about some of the things that had happened to her, in response to which they brought my parents into the room and told them that they were in a cult and must leave for the safety of their children. My sister moved out and never returned home.

The group did not stop us from leaving but surveilled us over time. When I was a teenager, my former sexual abuser stalked me at my job for three years, which angered my mom so much that she would wait in the parking lot holding a bat. I had ten reproductive surgeries, one of which removed scar tissue so that I could have my only child, who is now grown at eighteen years of age and transcribing for me, hearing some of these things for the first time as we write this chapter together. Subsequently, I had a full hysterectomy. My older sister was not so lucky and has never been able to give birth.

By the time we left the cult, I was experiencing dissociative identity disorder (DID). I was eventually triggered into episodes that would leave no question that I had unresolved trauma. Consequently, I got a brain scan at the Doctor Amen clinic that would show the classic diamond, as they called it, which was evidence of posttraumatic stress disorder (PTSD) along with a brain injury from a small piercing object that had entered my skull right between my eyes. I followed up by receiving eye movement desensitization and reprocessing therapy (EMDR), as well as counseling in another state for satanic ritual abuse (SRA), in which I was amazed at the amount of people with similar stories and damage.

It wasn't until I got sober through a twelve-step program that I was able to complete the recovery process and fully heal eight years ago. Through this process, I came to embrace my higher power. I started to experience a broad road to freedom in which my past, my hate, and my disdain no longer controlled me. I came to the understanding that everyone is human and in need of grace.

When we are of sane and sound mind, we can do what needs to be done and separate the facts from our feelings. This allows us to become a part of the solution in every situation rather than a part of the problem. It also situates us to share our experience, strength, and hope for those who need it. Today, my primary purpose is clear: to help others who are still suffering. In turn, the right question becomes, "How can I help?" As a result, I saw the opportunity to share my story as a blessing. I've found that the greatest detriment to our ability to thrive is the shadow of secrecy. Like plants, we need light to grow.

The composition of this chapter comes in good time, though I am not accustomed to talking about this part of my story anymore. I don't live in these events, and they don't control me. It is said that the abuser abuses you once, but you abuse yourself a thousand times. Only when you fully heal does the experience truly end.

—Mary, May 2024

PUZZLE PIECES

- How does Mary's story challenge stereotypes about the types of families who can become entangled in abusive groups or cults?

- What role did secrecy play in keeping the abuse hidden in Mary's family?
- How might Mary's resilience and healing journey influence the way society views survivors?
- What safeguards—legal, medical, or community based—could prevent families from being drawn into harmful groups like the one Mary described?
- How does Mary's reflection that "the greatest detriment to our ability to thrive is the shadow of secrecy" resonate beyond her story?

Chapter 11

BUDDY

At the end of 2014, there were over 2.1 million protection orders entered in state repositories and more than 1.4 million entered in federal databases.[1]

On December 16, 2013, I met and consulted with Buddy Webb. He had been served notice that his ex-wife, Lori Beth Schlagal, was seeking a protective order against him. I quoted him the retainer required if he wanted me to represent him at the hearing, which was scheduled to take place only forty-eight hours from the time of this first consultation.

The next day, Buddy retained me to be his lawyer. Then, on December 18, 2013, my co-counsel, Luke Gunnstaks, and I were in court before Judge Dean Rucker, defending Buddy on this request for a protective order. Lori was represented by the Midland County District Attorney's Office. She was claiming she needed this protection because her ex-husband, Buddy, had sent her two emails almost a year apart. She claimed she felt "harassed."

The hearing began at 10:33 a.m. and was over at 1:36 p.m. The court recessed for a lunch break from 12:08 p.m. to 1:01 p.m. According to the time stamp on the court reporter's transcript, the entire hearing lasted two hours and ten minutes. At the conclusion of the testimony, Judge Rucker said he would let us know his ruling in the next few days.

On January 13, 2014, Judge Rucker signed a final protective order against Webb. The period of time for the length of this protective order was for the *lifetime* of Buddy or Lori, whoever died first. Webb, by this order, was stripped of his right to own or possess a gun, and he was branded for life as a stalker.

There were never any criminal charges brought against him, nor was he convicted of any charges. He was not given the right to a trial by jury. He merely showed up to defend himself against his ex-wife, who was claiming she felt harassed by his two emails.

While we ordered the transcript and appealed this ruling, the Eastland Court of Appeals upheld Judge Dean Rucker's ruling.

I include this chapter about Webb in this book because I believe it is important for the reader to know how harshly and quickly a ruling came down in Midland County, Texas—a ruling that forever altered and changed Webb's life. His marriage to Lori Schlagal only lasted three months before they separated, and they divorced three months after that.

I am including excerpts of the brief we filed on Buddy's behalf before the Eastland Court of Appeals, which sets out the statement of facts as developed in the hearing. For those who want to review all of the briefs, arguments, and opinion, they are available in No. 11-14-00101-CV in the Eleventh Court of Appeals of Eastland, Texas.

There is another aspect of Webb and his story that is not reflected in the hearing transcript on December 18, 2013, nor in the briefs filed before the Eastland Court or the Texas Supreme Court.

It has now been more than ten years since I was in court with Webb. Before I wrote this chapter, I called and asked Buddy for permission to share some things about this protective order hearing and the appeal. Buddy gave me permission. He also shared with me the fact that he has developed quite a following on his internet blogs and postings. Buddy is a computer expert and had video surveillance cameras installed throughout his home before he was shot by an intruder. Buddy is prolific in describing various events, facts, observations, and theories about what is going on in Midland County, Texas. He told me he has had over 1.2 million hits to his YouTube Channel, where he addresses issues of sex trafficking and corruption in his postings.

I have never gone to Buddy's website, but I came to know Buddy while working as his attorney. I found him to be a gentle, kind, highly intelligent man who was asking some questions of his ex-wife, and what he got in response was a lifetime protective order.

Here is a portion of the brief we filed:

STATEMENT OF FACTS

Applicant Lori Beth Schlagal ("Lori," "Applicant," or "Appellee") and Respondent Buddy Wayne Webb ("Buddy," "Respondent," or "Appellant") are former spouses. (2 RR 10). They separated in December of 2011 after three months of marriage. (2 RR 11). They have no children together. (2 RR 11). They were divorced after about six months, on March 26, 2012, on the ground of insupportability. (RR 11; SCR ___). There were no findings of family violence reflected in the parties' Final Decree of Divorce, which both parties agreed to and signed. (SCR___). However, on November 26, 2013, Lori filed an Application for Protective Order against Buddy pursuant to Chapter 7A of the Texas Code of Criminal Procedure for herself and her minor daughter from a previous marriage, K.C., age 14, alleging that they are the victims of stalking. (CR 6-14).

Buddy is disabled. (2 RR 12). On January 28, 2012, while the parties were separated but still married, an intruder shot Buddy in the foot while in his Midland home, inflicting a massive and disabling gunshot wound. (2 RR 11-12; R. Exh. 2). Three months after he was shot, Buddy and Lori divorced, and the last time Buddy had seen or talked to Lori prior to seeing her in Court on December 18, 2013, occurred in June or July of 2012. (2 RR 26-27).

Buddy has tried desperately to get law enforcement to thoroughly investigate the gunshot incident, and in fact, when Assistant District Attorney Stacey Jewett ("ADA Jewett") called Buddy to notify him of the Application for Protective Order filed against him, Buddy testified that he had actually been excited, thinking that "justice was coming," and that surely she was calling to let him know that this case (as a crime victim) was finally moving forward.(2 RR 41-42). But the purpose of ADA Jewett's call to Buddy was far removed from the justice he had so desired.

Instead, Buddy was being accused of stalking Lori and her minor daughter from a previous marriage, K.C. Even though Buddy thought that Lori had been living and was still living in Lubbock, Lori alleges in her Application that "there is a clear and present danger of stalking." (2 RR 27; 2 RR 45). However, it wasn't until Buddy received Lori's Application for Protective Order that he first learned that Lori was not living in Lubbock, and he testified he did not have her phone number (2RR 27; 2 RR 45).

He had no idea that she had returned to Midland; he had not seen or spoken to her for a year and a half; and he had not had her phone number for years. (2RR 27; 2RR 45). As for Lori's daughter K.C., Buddy testified that he had not seen her in more than two years. (2 RR 43).

Lori, however, would have the court believe that she is a victim of stalking, on the basis of the following allegations:

1). The Room "Incident"—In her sworn affidavit, Lori alleges that, in December of 2011, while they were still married, Buddy locked her inside a room for over a twenty-four hour period during which she alleges that he accused her of, and questioned her about, various criminal dealings, including "the disappearance of his pistol." (CR 12). During the protective order hearing, however, she changed her previously sworn-to testimony to say that Buddy was not outside the room while she was locked inside; rather, Lori and Buddy were actually both inside of the room, a dramatically different scenario. (2 RR 71).

Regardless, Buddy denies both of Lori's "versions" of her story, and in fact he unequivocally denies that this incident ever occurred at all. (2 RR 36). And despite her dramatic recount of this alleged incident in a lone paragraph within her supporting affidavit, there was no police report or other credible evidence, documentary or otherwise, of this alleged incident nor reference to it anywhere during the divorce proceedings. (2 RR 72;2 RR 77).

Furthermore, she had never sought a Title 4 Protective Order under the Texas Family Code or reported any family violence. (2 RR 77). She had never pursued any criminal charges for unlawful restraint or terroristic threats. (2 RR 77). In fact, she had never even brought such a bizarre and extreme story to any court's attention until a full two years after the alleged incident occurred and after a divorce had been granted in which she failed to raise any such allegations or requests for relief related thereto. (CR 12).

2). Two Emails—Buddy sent Lori two emails. He sent her one email on November 8, 2012, and one email over a year later on October 6, 2013. (2 RR 68). In both emails to Lori, Buddy is legitimately seeking information from Lori about his own victimization when he had been shot by an intruder in his own home. In his November 8, 2012, email, Buddy wants Lori to contact the FBI if she has any information, or if she is withholding any information, as might be the case, about Buddy being shot. (State Exh. 2). Lori testified that the emails contain no threats. (2 RR 85).

Although Lori testified that she "reported" the first email to the police, this is not actually the case. The evidence adduced at trial revealed that Detective Rosie Rodriguez, a police investigator working Buddy's gunshot case, was actually trying to get in touch with *Lori* about *Buddy* mysteriously being shot in the leg on January 28, 2012, and it was actually at this point in time that Lori brought up to Detective Rosie Rodriguez ("Detective Rodriguez") that Buddy had sent her an email. (2 RR 55).

However, Detective Rodriguez never made any police report, call log, or other report regarding Buddy's alleged "harassment" via email of Lori. (2RR 57-58). Detective Rodriguez testified that she never saw any harassing emails, even though she requested to see the emails from Lori. (2 RR

59-62). When the State showed her the two emails in State's Exhibits 1 and 2, Detective Rodriguez testified that she had not seen those.

(2 RR 64). Detective Rodriguez further testified that she never saw any evidence that Buddy was somehow stalking Lori. (2 RR 62). And Detective Rodriguez testified that she never saw anything that would evidence family violence. (2 RR 62).

Although Lori swears that she sent some sort of "cease and desist"–type email to Buddy on the advice of Detective Rodriguez, allegedly stating that Lori did not want Buddy to contact her again, Lori admits that she does not have this allegedly important email—a seemingly critical piece of her case—to offer into evidence. (2 RR 67-68; 2 RR 73-74). Buddy denies ever receiving any such communication from Lori, and he testifies that he did not know that Lori had any issue with him contacting her "until he got this order." (2 RR 36).

3). Facebook—In what could be the social media equivalent of "the telephone game," Lori's affidavit provides a gossipy account via inadmissible (quadruple!) hearsay that in October of 2013, Buddy was allegedly posting threats on Facebook that he was going to kill Lori. However, although Lori's supporting affidavit to her Application for Protective Order indicates the time frame of the alleged Facebook posting "incident" as October of 2013, she provided conflicting testimony at the protective order hearing that the alleged Facebook posting "incident" allegedly occurred instead in December of 2013. (2 RR 89-90).

This is both nonsensical and impossible, since the Application for Protective Order was filed, and a Temporary

Ex Parte Protective Order and Show Cause Order signed, on November 26, 2013. (CR 14-19). However, Lori has no personal, firsthand knowledge of these alleged posts. She has never obtained any proof or even seen any evidence of these alleged posts. (2 RR 77). And she brought no documentary evidence of these alleged posts to the evidentiary hearing on her application for a stalking protective order. (2 RR 77). The following excerpt of her testimony regarding the alleged Facebook threats reveals the scurrilous nature of the accusations against Buddy:

Q. Where is this supposed posting that Buddy was threatening to kill you?

A. Let me—I'll tell you what has happened.

Q. No. No. Where is it?

A. I can't answer that.

Q. It doesn't exist. You haven't been able to track down such a document, have you?

A. Personally, no.

Q. And all these people who are telling you about it, they can't even produce it, can they?

A. I don't know. I can't answer your question. (2 RR 77).

Lori could not show the trial court one example of the alleged Facebook threats against her because there were none. Buddy never wrote any such post. (2 RR 47). What he did do, however, was *privately* respond through Facebook to an unsolicited message from Lori's former boyfriend, Arthur Welch, who sent Buddy a *private* Facebook message asking Buddy if *Lori* had anything to do with *Buddy* getting shot . . . because evidently, according to Arthur, Lori had threatened to have Arthur killed once upon a time. (2 RR 47-48; R. Exh. 3).

Buddy Wayne Webb is a man that was mysteriously shot in the leg in his own home. A former boyfriend of Lori's contacted Buddy out of the blue and expressly suggested that Lori could have been involved. (2 RR 48). Naturally, Buddy had some questions for Lori after he received this disturbing information, and Buddy sent her two emails over a year apart to inquire about her involvement, which would clearly be within his First Amendment right to do so, and would also be consistent with his belief that the District Attorney was still investigating his own case in which he was the victim of a shooting.

As a result of Buddy exercising his right to freedom of speech, he was hauled into court and slapped with a permanent [emphasis added] Protective Order, replete with far-reaching consequences and grave stigma, forever prohibiting him from communicating with former family members, even if those persons could have valuable information relevant to his own case in which he was the victim of a shooting, going "near" or within 200 yards of where Lori or K.C. might possibly be, forever prohibiting him from ever owning any firearm or ammunition, permanently suspending any concealed handgun license, putting Midland law enforcement on notice of the protective order against him, and permanently violating his constitutional rights guaranteed to all law-abiding citizens by the Constitutions of the United States of America and the State of Texas. (CR 47-53).

PUZZLE PIECES

- Why did Buddy's ex-wife feel threatened when Buddy asked if she knew anything about why he was shot in his home and whether she knew anything about his mother's death?
- Why do you think Judge Dean Rucker issued a lifetime protective order against Buddy without criminal charges or a jury trial?
- Who do you think shot Buddy?
- Why do you think Buddy's ex-wife accused him of stalking after he sent just two emails? Does that seem like a reasonable accusation?
- What does this ruling by Midland Judge Dean Rucker tell you when the same judge denied a protective order for a child when her father was sleeping naked with her in chapter 6? Or when this same judge gave the father full unsupervised access in the case of Gee described in chapter 4?
- Is this protective order an attempt to attack Buddy's credibility in his effort to discover and prosecute the person or persons behind Buddy being shot in his own home?
- Is this protective order an attempt to attack Buddy's credibility in calling for an investigation of sex trafficking in Midland, Texas?
- Do you want to know more about Buddy Webb or underground tunnels? Check out his YouTube Channel.

Chapter 12

CHIEF OF POLICE GOES TO FEDERAL PRISON FOR CHILD PORNOGRAPHY

Child pornography made up 69 percent of sex offenses referred to US attorneys in 2006.[1]

On May 3, 2001, I was hired by the wife of the chief of police in Odessa, Texas, to represent her in a divorce. They had no children born of their marriage, so the issues before the court involved property division only.

Not long into my representation of Mrs. Jenkins against her husband, James Jenkins, she revealed to me that her husband was regularly accessing child pornography on his computer when he was at home. Furthermore, he had acquired a new computer and had left the hard drive from the old computer at their house when he vacated the marital residence. She explained that he had attempted to delete everything on the old hard drive, but she believed there was still child porn on it. She brought this old hard drive to my office and left it with me.

Oh my gosh! I had to make some wise decisions very quickly. If what my client was telling me was true (and, as it turned out, it *was* true), I was holding some evidence that needed to be turned over to the proper authorities immediately. I can't hold or possess such materials. It is illegal to be in possession of child pornography, even if it is evidence in a divorce case. This was somewhat the equivalent of being in possession of heroin or cocaine. All of it is illegal to possess.

Obviously, I couldn't turn it in to the Odessa Police Department. James Jenkins was the chief of police for Odessa. I had even sued this man in federal court in 1993, when he first came to Odessa. That case was brought on behalf of Barbara Gillis, the top-ranking officer in the Odessa Police Department at the time Jenkins arrived. His abuse and harassment of Deputy Chief Gillis, as shown in official court filings, resulted in a quick settlement by the City of Odessa paying $140,000 for his actions and violations.

From the time we filed the lawsuit for Officer Gillis until the case was settled was only a matter of days. My first impression of Chief James Jenkins was not favorable in the least. My first opinions of him were only validated and strengthened by this new revelation that he liked to hang out on child porn sites.

In early 2001, there were two federal agencies that investigated and dealt with child pornography: the FBI and US Customs. I didn't know whom James Jenkins knew and what his connections were with any of them. If I called the local FBI office and turned this over to them, would they merely sweep it under the rug or hand the hard drive back to him? I didn't know who the good guys were and who the bad guys were.

I just prayed really hard that God would lead me to the right person in the agency who would truly investigate this situation to determine whether what my client was telling me was true. I decided to start with the US Marshal's Office in Houston, Texas, a ten-hour drive away from Odessa. Maybe they wouldn't be too connected or buddies with the Odessa chief of police.

The person I talked to in Houston referred me to someone in Austin, Texas. I called that agency in Austin and explained again who I was, what I had, and what I was trying to do. That person referred me to a man named Jim Coleman in San Angelo, Texas, with the US Customs Office. Since I really hadn't dealt with these kinds of circumstances before, I was a little surprised that there was a US Customs Office in San Angelo, a town only a two-and-a-half-hour drive from Odessa.

Coleman listened to me explain what I had and who I was dealing with. At the end of our conversation, he told me he would be at my office in three hours to take possession of the hard drive. When Agent Coleman showed up, he was wearing cowboy boots and a cowboy hat. I guess I just hadn't dealt with federal Customs agents enough to know what their uniforms looked like, but this was at least consistent with the San Angelo rancher style of dress I remembered from my childhood experiences of being there with my grandparents, who had a sheep ranch in nearby Coleman County.

I immediately trusted Agent Coleman and shared with him what my client had told me about the hard drive and her husband's activities of regularly surfing child porn sites. Agent Coleman listened carefully and respectfully. He understood the nature of my client's and my position in turning over evidence that could lead to a federal felony indictment and imprisonment if it were true.

I felt sure that Agent Coleman was light-years ahead of me on what to do in an investigation like this, but he listened to me as

I made a couple of suggestions. First of all, I thought that Chief Jenkins might claim he was working some type of task force on child pornography and that anything on the computer was a part of his investigation. Agent Coleman told me he would check it out, which he did. There was no agency working with Chief Jenkins or the Odessa Police Department on a child pornography task force.

The other defense I thought Chief Jenkins might make was that my client was trying to set him up—that *she* was the one going to child porn sites on her husband's computer. Agent Coleman let me know later that the US Customs agents covered that possible angle as well.

They had obtained the airline tickets documenting when my client had gone to Florida to visit her daughters. She was away from Odessa and away from the computer, yet the illegal activities continued. Since the forensic analysis done by the US Customs agents could identify every keystroke of the computer and the date, they knew Jim Jenkins continued to access the child porn sites while his wife was in Florida.

We waited for the federal agents to do their job and analysis. In late August or early September 2001, I received a call from Agent Coleman. He told me he was calling to let me know something would be happening soon, just to let my client be prepared. Beyond that, we didn't know what it was or when it would happen.

Then, September 11, 2001, happened, the day that shook our country to its core. On that Tuesday, I wasn't thinking about Chief James Jenkins or his computer hard drive. Like most Americans, I was in shock and deeply disturbed by the attacks in New York, Washington, DC, and Pennsylvania. I believe most of us were trying to figure out whether we were about to go to war, whether there would be more attacks, what was going on, and what would happen next.

Amid the most tragic events that week, on Thursday, September 13, 2001, a local news story broke. Chief of Police James Jenkins had suddenly resigned from the Odessa Police Department. There was no explanation forthcoming from James Jenkins. The reporters for the local TV stations and the *Odessa American* reported the resignation, but they were at a loss for the chief's reason for resigning.[2]

I suppose the reporters didn't know what else to write about him, so they wrote glowing reports recapping his wonderful work in Odessa. They commented how great he was on programs working with children! I think they even overlooked that nasty little federal lawsuit when he arrived in town and mistreated Deputy Chief Gillis.[3]

Then, on Friday afternoon, September 14, 2001, James Jenkins appeared in federal court in Midland, Texas, and entered his guilty plea for child pornography. In that single appearance, he went from being the highly praised chief of police to being a convicted felon.[4]

On Saturday morning, September 15, 2001, the very top of the first page of the *Odessa American* bumped the spot usually reserved for high school football scores and ran the following headline: "Ex-Chief Pleads Guilty to Child Porn."[5]

It was several weeks before James Jenkins was sentenced to eighteen months in federal prison. At the end of the year, the *Odessa American* ranked their top ten stories of the year.[6] The number one story was about our chief of police going to federal prison, the number two story was the tragedy of September 11th and the Twin Towers being hit, and the number three story was local hometown boy George W. Bush being sworn in as president of the United States.

Upon his federal conviction, James Howard Jenkins became a registered sex offender for the rest of his life. My client moved away, and I never heard from her again after the divorce was granted.

I have three plaques hanging in my office hallway of the newspaper articles regarding my dealings with James Jenkins. The first one is the 1993 case in which we sued him for his abusive conduct toward Barbara Gillis. The other two are regarding his guilty plea and the newspaper rating it the number one story of the year.

I walk by these plaques every day when I go to the front reception room to bring a client back to my office or to speak to my legal assistant. They are reminders to me that I am making a difference in the world of justice, even as a West Texas divorce lawyer.

PUZZLE PIECES

- What do you make of Odessa's own chief of police going to federal prison for accessing child pornography?
- Why do you think it was necessary to contact someone outside of Odessa to investigate the contents of the hard drive?
- What do you think would have happened if Attorney Clack had gone directly to the Odessa police with the hard drive?
- Why do you think the chief's scandal ranked as the year's biggest local story, even above a national tragedy and a presidential inauguration? What does that say about the impact of betrayal close to home?
- What do you think would have happened if Attorney Clack's plan had backfired and Agent Coleman had taken the hard drive directly to the Odessa police instead of investigating matters further?

- Why do you think Attorney Clack fights so hard for justice in her community? Are you noticing any patterns in these puzzle pieces?
- Are you becoming familiar with any names or noticing any connections between any of the cases you've read thus far?

Chapter 13

ALLEGATIONS OF COACHING

In 2020, during the COVID-19 pandemic, Texas Child Protective Services received more than 278,000 reports of child abuse or neglect. Pandemic-related disruptions and staff shortages contributed to significant delays in investigations and case processing across the state.[1]

Beginning in March 2020, everything about the way I ran my office changed, just as it did for most the people in our country. The COVID-19 pandemic had begun, and none of us fully realized at the beginning what was in store. We were keeping our distance, trying to stay healthy, wearing masks, and checking our temperatures when arriving at work. We continued coming into the office, but we were relying on Zoom calls to communicate hearings being conducted over computer monitors. We were eating our lunches at our desks, away from others at the office, and everyone was stocking up on toilet paper.

Schools had shut down around spring break in March 2020. As far as in-person attendance, children in this part of Texas, and probably most of the country, were finishing their school year remotely.

By June 2020, we were adapting to our new safety protocols. I needed to stay healthy for myself and my employees. If I became ill or unable to practice law, my solo law practice would collapse. I also had to consider the health of my ninety-two-year-old mother, who lived two doors down from me, and my longtime boyfriend, who lived with me. Randall and I had been together for years. He was my main private investigator and the father of our adult daughter we'd adopted together, and he also had a diagnosis in the summer of 2018 of stage 4 prostate cancer. Even with his serious health challenges, Randall had continued working as a PI until COVID-19 hit. I was still going into the office, but all of our lives had changed dramatically.

It was during the pandemic that I was contacted by another lawyer to help him on a particularly disturbing and difficult divorce case pending in Midland, Texas. Although this lawyer was also a board-certified family law specialist, there were things about the case he just didn't understand. He wanted to bring me on board to sit second chair and take about three depositions. He wanted to run these facts by me, get my input and suggestions, and just assist with what was about to explode into twenty-four depositions and a massive amount of discovery: requests for production, interrogatories, and requests for admission.

The lawyer on the opposing side was Brad Miller, a lawyer who was of counsel in Hal Brockett's office. The judge was David Lindemood, also formerly of counsel in Brockett's office. I could already tell this was going to be tough, and I agreed to talk to the client.

On June 3, 2020, I met the wife, who I'm going to refer to as Janice. I'm also going to refer to her two sons as Joseph and Jacob and her husband as Jay. When I met Janice, the boys were ages seven and five.

Janice came to my office along with her parents. She explained she had discovered the previous August that her husband was gay. She had found out when she stumbled across a Facebook exchange between Jay and his boyfriend, Dan, who lived in Houston. The dialogue was quite vulgar and descriptive of their bondage and sadistic conduct with each other. When Janice had confronted Jay about this discovery, he wanted to continue his relationship with Dan and move Dan into their house in Midland. Jay's proposal was that he and Janice would stay married as a cover but that he and Dan would continue with their relationship in the privacy of the marital home. Janice would basically be their maid and cook but continue being Jay's wife in name only. Janice immediately turned down Jay's proposed arrangement and filed for divorce.

Janice was a graduate of law school and had a law license that she had allowed to go inactive once she and Jay had started their family and she became a stay-at-home mom. She also had a few insurance clients through her dad's agency in a town near Houston. Jay had held his job for thirteen years with the same company. He had been transferred to Midland from Houston a couple of years before Janice discovered the affair. Jay was a computer expert, had an MBA, and held a responsible position in his company in the oil and gas industry. Jay traveled a lot during the week conducting training programs and presentations.

At their temporary hearing in September 2019, the only issue in dispute was regarding a geographic restriction. Janice wanted to be free to move back to the Houston area with the children. Jay had agreed she would be primary custodian of the children, and they agreed he would have a standard possession order. Jay had moved out of the family home and was living in a travel trailer outside the city limits of Midland. This trailer was where he had the children during his visitation with them.

Janice had no relatives in the Midland–Odessa area. She had some acquaintances and friends through the First Baptist Church in Midland, and she had joined Junior League, a women's service and social organization. Janice really wanted to get back to the Houston area, where she had family and lifelong friends. She needed and wanted her support group.

Jay, however, fought her on this issue, and Judge Jeff Robnett, another district judge at the Midland Courthouse, denied Janice's request to move away from Midland. Now she would have to stay in Midland with her two boys even though she had no job and no support group.

I asked Janice about Jay's parents and where they lived and what they did for a living. She explained they had a ranch in Oklahoma, and they had horses. They even had disadvantaged children come to their ranch to ride those horses.

How nice, I thought.

"Did they inherit this ranch?" I asked.

"No."

"How did they acquire it?"

Janice explained that Jay's mom had been the school secretary at an elementary school in Oklahoma, and his dad had been a welder for the same company where Jay had worked for the last thirteen years. Her father-in-law listed his job as construction support on LinkedIn.

I asked whether Jay's parents had any other resources or money to buy a ranch, buy horses, feed the animals, maintain the acreage and fences, and afford all the expenses involved in owning a ranch and horses. Janice said they had told her they had invested well, but no, they didn't have any other jobs, trust funds, or other known sources of income.

I had some knowledge about the cost of running and maintaining a ranch and horses from representing some clients over the years who have those kinds of assets. I know it costs a whole lot of money to sustain this lifestyle—a lot more than a school secretary and welder would be earning.

Janice continued with her story of why she was considering adding me to her legal team. After the first hearing, she was taking the children to a couple of counselors connected to the First Baptist Church. The children were acting out during bath time in a very sexual manner toward each other. She had discussed this with the counselors and sought their recommendations as to how to deal with her sons' inappropriate behavior. The counselors reported the boys' actions to Child Protective Services (CPS) since they were mandatory reporters.

When the two lawyers she first hired to file the divorce (a husband-and-wife team) found out these two counselors had notified CPS, they told Janice it was a mistake to call CPS, as boys would be boys. They said she would lose her boys now if she didn't contact the counselor and retract what the boys had said. It was at that point Janice dismissed their services and hired the board-certified lawyer who, months later, contacted me.

Because CPS had been contacted and a report had been filed indicating inappropriate conduct, including statements by the children, who were four and six at the time, a CPS worker showed up to meet with Janice and the boys. Her sons had told Janice that they'd learned their bathtub behavior from the video they had seen at

Daddy's. A forensic interview was set up to interview the children at the Midland Children's Advocacy Center (CAC), but there was a lapse of over fourteen days from the time CPS and the parents were notified and the interview took place.

When Jay was notified that the children were acting out sexually with each other and that a report had been made to CPS, Jay proceeded with his Thanksgiving visitation with the children as scheduled. He took them to his parents' ranch in Oklahoma for nine days. When the boys got back to Midland and went to their forensic interview, Joseph, the six-year-old, "didn't want to talk about it." And Jacob, the four-year-old, didn't have much to say, but at the end, he did say that Daddy took a picture of his private area with his phone, the "Texas" one, and "then put it in the trash." Jay had two cell phones. He had one with an Oklahoma area code and one with a Texas area code.

When the CPS worker came out of the forensic interview, Janice was informed that the children had nothing to report and didn't want to talk. This was on December 4, 2019. Janice has not seen this taped interview of the children to this day, but she was disturbed that CPS had delayed so long in getting the interview set up. What happened in Oklahoma during those nine days that Joseph was not wanting to talk about?

Since Janice was concerned that the children's actions might be an indication something inappropriate was going on, she decided to take the children to a more qualified counselor. She chose Tommy Pool, a licensed professional counselor with a master's degree. Mr. Pool worked with children and adults. His office was in Odessa, and he seemed to be well respected by attorneys and judges in the Odessa and Midland area. He was often appointed by judges in the area to work with children and families. Judge Sara Kate Billingsley, the district judge for the 446th Judicial District Court in Odessa, had for a certain period of time ordered all parents with minor children going through divorce or custody litigation in her court to attend a parenting class taught by Pool. Eager to understand what was happening, Janice made appointments for her children to start seeing Pool.

In January 2020, Joseph, the elder child, told his mother that Daddy had touched his "winkie." He said it had happened at the trailer. Joseph also made statements along those lines to Pool. Again, CPS was notified. Janice's new lawyer filed a motion, requesting an emergency hearing asking that Jay's visitation with the children cease or that it be only under the supervision of a court-appointed monitor.

This was the second time Joseph had made a statement to Janice during bath time about this behavior. She got Joseph out of the bathtub and decided to try to get him to say it again in their living room, where she had a Ring video camera on the mantel above the fireplace. Her parents had only recently given her this camera because someone had tried to break into her home after the divorce was filed. The camera was motion activated, so she wasn't sure it would record, but she felt she needed to try. She asked Joseph to say again what he had said moments earlier in the bathtub. Joseph again made the statement about Daddy touching his private area.

The CPS worker assigned to the case was a young woman named Elise Butterfield, who had been working there for three or four months. She was in a probationary period as a caseworker because she was still in training. She showed up the next day at Joseph's school after Pool made his report. According to Butterfield's report, Joseph again stated Daddy had touched his private area. Ms. Butterfield arranged for both children to go to a forensic interview at the CAC right away. They interviewed Joseph, and this time, he talked. He said Daddy had touched him.

The following are excerpts from Butterfield's investigation report, including the child's statements and the counselors' statements, dated February 12, 2020:*

- The child reported to me this date that his father had touched his bare "winky" (penis) on numerous occasions. He demonstrated this candidly by putting his hand down into his own pants, stating, "He touches me down there a lot. I'm usually laying down in bed in my PJs because we sleep in the same bed." He said that his father did this as recently as his last visit, which was apparently on the weekend of 2-7-20 – 2-9-20.
- Joseph reported that his father had perpetrated sexual assault on him numerous times over the last several custodial visits.
- The child reported to me that he was afraid to talk about what happened to him, but he was willing to talk to me and did tell me the things I have written. I believe there may be more abuse than the child has said thus far because of this.
- Joseph brought up an incident "when Daddy was trying to kill Mom because she had jaw surgery."
- I asked if he could tell me what he calls those parts and he stated "winky" and "bottom." I asked Joseph if someone has ever touched him on his private parts and he stated his dad touched him. MI [master investigator] Martinez asked what

----

* These excerpts were written as bullet points in Butterfield's report just as they've been presented here.

he meant and asked if it was over clothes or under clothes. Joseph stated it was under clothes and it happened once. MI Martinez asked if he knew why his daddy touched him, and Joseph stated he does not know why.

- I informed MI Christiaans that I had just finished speaking to Joseph, and he did make an outcry that his father touched his "winky" under his clothes and did not know why he touched him.
- My Daddy touched my private part, my penis.
- "Every single thing, step-by-step, like how you told me about your day today. Tell me everything that happened right before he touched your penis," At this point, Joseph was lying on the floor while speaking to Ms. Shores [a person present during the interview]. Joseph stated, "He was pulling my pants down. He touched my winky. That's all." Ms. Shores asked Joseph where Joseph was at "when he pulled your pants down." Joseph had rolled away on the floor and mumbled something, and Ms. Shores stated she could not hear him because he had his face in the carpet. Joseph stated, "At his trailer." Ms. Shores verified if Joseph was referring to his dad's trailer, and Joseph confirmed he was. She asked Joseph, "Where at, at the trailer were you?" Joseph responded he was in the living room, the couch with the bed, and he was sleeping.
- "And what part of your winky was he touching?" Joseph stated, "Where I pee."

Of course, Janice was not present in the room during the children's interview. She did not know what they'd said to the person asking the questions. When Joseph came out, Janice asked her son how he'd done. The following is an excerpt from the CPS report by Butterfield dated February 12, 2020. I have replaced the actual name of my client with *Janice* in this report:

> Detective Rogers [from Midland Police Department] brought up the previous CPS case from December 2019. It was brought up that her son had seen a picture of her husband's penis while she was sending it to her lawyer. Detective Rogers stated he did not know why she [Janice] was not in jail for that because "that is giving a child access to pornographic material. Whether he happened to see it over your shoulder or not, you did not take the proper precautions to ensure that child did not see the photo." He also mentioned the reason Janice was not in handcuffs at this moment was because he could proved she showed her child the photo and right now he was giving her "the benefit of the doubt." Janice began to shed tears and became irate. It was explained that we do look back into case history and between this case and the previous one, the outcry that Joseph made does not appear to be genuine. It was stated by Det. Rogers, MI Martinez, and myself [Elise Butterfield] that statements made by the child sound "coached." I [Elise Butterfield] clarified that I was not saying that is what she did, but the outcry does not sound genuine. Det. Rogers stated that he noticed on another camera—in the room where Janice had been waiting with Jacob while Joseph was interviewed—she asked Joseph what he said and he told her "same as last time." Det. Rogers stated, "That right there, convinces me he's being coached." Janice stated that she did

not know how to prove that she was not lying or telling the child what to say.

On February 28, 2020, Janice went to court on her request to modify Jay's access to the children. Jay testified that he had never touched the children, that what Janice was saying was a lie, and that the children were lying. Pool testified as to what Joseph had told him and that he believed Joseph was telling the truth. Pool did not believe the children had been coached by Janice.

At the end of the hearing before Judge David Lindemood, the judge ordered a complete change in the custody order. Jay was named as temporary sole managing conservator, and Janice would only see the children while being supervised at Centers for Children and Families in two-hour visits a couple of times per month. The judge said he thought Janice had coached the children, although the CAC interview was not played to the judge.

He also ordered both parents to submit to a psychological exam and testing before Dr. Perry Marchioni and for that report to be completed and back to him by a certain date. The children were to be turned over to Dad immediately. It was about two weeks later that the COVID-19 shutdown happened. Janice went seventy-eight days without seeing her children at all.

She submitted to the psychological testing by Dr. Marchioni, as did Jay. The reports came back. Janice's came back as fairly normal for a mother going through this kind of stressful litigation. In Dr. Marchioni's report dated April 2, 2020, he noted that Jay described that he was not gay and was not dating, was denying homosexuality, and had issues of anger management. Dr. Marchioni also recommended in his report that Jay should attend anger management classes and that the investigation into allegations of sexual abuse needed to be examined carefully. Those allegations would need to be cleared in order to determine their impact on whether Jay could have unsupervised contact with his children.

The board-certified lawyer representing Janice filed for another hearing before Judge Lindemood asking that he reconsider his prior ruling in light of the Marchioni report. Lindemood refused to turn the children back over to Mom. What he did do was give her a few unsupervised hours on Saturday and a few hours on Sunday twice per month. But there were no overnights with Mom.

This is a summary of the case as it had developed leading up to this June 3, 2020, appointment with Janice and her parents. They were confused. They didn't understand why the judge was doing this, especially with the children making outcries and with the negative things about Jay in the Dr. Marchioni report. The lawyer who was representing them and asked me to join the case was a very conservative, religious man, and he didn't understand why the judge was ruling the way he was.

I had been listening carefully to this mother and her parents. They were God-loving people who were very strong in their Baptist beliefs and teachings. Janice's granddaddy was a Baptist preacher who had performed her marriage ceremony to Jay in October 2010.

As I sat there talking to these folks, I was deciding whether to tell them what I really thought about this case and what I thought was going on. After some back-and-forth, I decided I might as well tell this woman and her parents what I really thought we were confronting and said, "I think you are dealing with The Club. It is not 'the good old boys' club.' It is not the country club." I explained that I had been seeing things of a disturbing nature since 1995, when I had worked on a big contested custody case in Midland.

Obviously, Judge Lindemood did not like or believe Janice and what she was reporting. If she was to have any chance of getting her boys back, she was going to have to pay the jury fee ($40), request a jury trial, and go before twelve citizens in Midland. She was going to have to win the jury trial. I told her the fee needed to be paid immediately and that it would probably be a very long, hard, and expensive battle. I told her, "It may cost you hundreds of thousands of dollars, but it is your only chance, as I see it, to get your boys back. Judge Lindemood doesn't look like he's going to rule in your favor at all."

They retained me to come on board and sit second chair, with their other lawyer to remain as lead counsel. The jury fee was paid. With all of the challenges of a terribly hard case and the new limitations of the COVID-19 pandemic protocol, we began working to try to get Janice's boys back. The fate of Janice's children would be in the hands of twelve jurors.

PUZZLE PIECES

- What do you think happened over the Thanksgiving visitation with Jay and his parents that made the boys not want to talk about the inappropriate conduct when they returned?
- Why do you think this judge flipped temporary sole managing conservatorship over to Jay after learning about the boy's outcry of sexual abuse by their father, especially when the counselor said he believed the child and did not see evidence of coaching?
- Why do you think Judge Lindemood disregarded the Marchioni report's concerns about Jay's anger and credibility,

accusing Janice and her sons of lying about the sexual abuse without even watching the video of the CAC interview?

- Do you see pieces of the puzzle consistent with Midland judges' rulings of not protecting children when they make outcries?

Chapter 14

PLACING THE CHILDREN WITH THE PREDATORS

"An estimated 58,000 US children are court ordered into the care of an abusing parent each and every year."[1]

From the time I joined the legal team as one of Janice's lawyers, I gave her my best advice and strategy suggestions. My ideas did not always match with what her lead counsel suggested. That is normal in my experience. I have been co-counsel with multiple lawyers over the years, and we have had spirited discussions on strategy and recommendations as to how to handle and go forward on the case. By October 2020, Janice's two lawyers were making such different recommendations that she had to make a decision regarding who would continue and see the case to its conclusion. She asked me to stay on and become lead counsel. I agreed to do that, provided Lane Haygood join my team as second chair and assist me through the jury trial.

Lane was a lawyer who rented office space in my building. He had grown up in Andrews, Texas, and was friends with my nephews. Lane had worked for my brother at his law office when he was in high school. Lane was a board-certified criminal appellate specialist, a highly intelligent lawyer, very good with the technological aspects in the courtroom, and a former prosecutor, and we were already working together on several of my other cases.

Lane agreed to join me in representing Janice. As we worked on her case, we were finding multiple examples of Jay perjuring himself. At first, he had testified under oath that he wasn't really gay, that it was only a one-time relationship with Dan. However, as we took depositions, we found more and more men with whom Jay was sexually involved.

Janice had hired a private investigator firm in Houston in which all of the private investigators were former FBI agents. They were able to track down other sexual partners of Jay's. When we took those depositions, some of these sexual partners testified under oath that they were meeting Jay on a phone app called Grindr, a hookup site for gay men. Jay's sworn testimony about these men differed from the men's sworn testimony. Jay didn't always know the last names of these guys. One man he listed as "unknown" for the name. They would hook up in the parking lot of the movie theater and have sex in Jay's vehicle and other random places. One sexual partner said they had met up as strangers at a trailer and started having sex within five minutes.

Jay was buying sexual devices from an online store in Georgia. We had the credit card receipts and the records of what Jay had purchased from the store. These were devices designed for inflicting pain and bondage. Jay finally testified, at the trial, that he kept a penis pump in the console of his company truck.

Jay lost his job in November 2020. Many people at the same company were laid off at the same time. Nevertheless, Jay and his lawyer maintained that Janice and her lawyers had caused him to lose his job. Jay's income for 2020 was around $170,000.

During the time that Jay had exclusive possession of the boys in the spring of 2020 and Janice did not see the boys at all, Joseph developed a condition called molluscum contagiosum. Later, Jacob developed it. The boys were treated for this condition by a Midland dermatologist. The wart-like bumps appeared in Joseph's genital area and over other parts of his body. They had to be burned off at multiple appointments, occurring over several months, at the doctor's office.

When Janice learned about this medical condition and researched it, she learned it can be sexually transmitted. Among children, it can also be spread on towels, such as at a swimming pool. This being the source of the condition was unlikely, though, since no swimming pools were open during the spring of 2020 because of the COVID-19 shutdown.

Janice was growing increasingly concerned that the children were being groomed to be sexually molested. While the divorce was pending, she attended a church concert in which Jacob was singing at First Baptist Church in Midland. Although they weren't really a happy family, they sat in the same row together for this church event. Jay had Joseph sitting in his lap, with Joseph facing him, pulling him in close, crotch to crotch. Janice was concerned that this position in public was a form of sexual grooming and that Jay was treating this position of pulling his son into his crotch as very normal and acceptable in this very public place.

We took Dr. Marchioni's deposition and asked him to give examples about conduct and patterns of sexually grooming a child. He confirmed that this kind of conduct exhibited by Jay at church could be a form of sexual grooming. I was having flashbacks of the video of the little twin girls in their supervised visitation at Centers, with Daddy getting on top of them, grinding and smelling their armpits and crotches. Here was Jay holding his older son in a very sexualized position at a church concert. When questioned about it, Jay acted like he was very innocent and that Janice was the one with the dirty mind.

After Jay lost his job with his company, he started working as a substitute schoolteacher. We were at a hearing about a month before the jury trial began when we learned that Jay had been banned from the Midland Independent School District (MISD) as a substitute. We asked Judge Lindemood for permission to reopen discovery so we could find out why Jay was banned from being a substitute. Judge Lindemood denied our request. We never learned why Jay was banned from MISD.

On May 17, 2021, we began jury selection for a one-week-long jury trial. When the trial began, Jay was the temporary sole managing conservator, the title Lindemood had given him fifteen months earlier when they had been at the temporary hearing on February 28, 2020. Janice had less time than standard visitation. Judge Lindemood had added two overnights per month, giving her Saturday morning to Sunday at 6:00 p.m. twice a month. Many witnesses testified in person and some by deposition. At the end of the trial and after their deliberation, the jury came back unanimously in favor of Janice, naming her as the permanent sole managing conservator of the boys. The jury also said Jay should pay Janice $100,000 in attorney's fees.

When Judge Lindemood had the hearing to announce his ruling on Jay's visitation, he gave Jay the maximum amount of time he could under the standard possession order. He gave Jay the "elections," which meant Jay got to pick the boys up from school when school was dismissed rather than wait until 6:00 p.m., and he got to return them to school on Monday mornings rather than return them at 6:00 p.m. on Sunday night. This expanded time frame gave Jay possession of the children approximately 44 percent of the time. The judge denied the $100,000 in attorneys' fees for Janice and said she could pay her own. The judge ordered that Jay pay child support based upon a minimum wage calculation of $7.25 per hour because he was unemployed. The Texas Family Code sets child support based upon the noncustodial parent's earning capacity if they are unemployed or underemployed. Judge Lindemood did not apply that provision based upon Jay's $170,000 income the prior year. Instead, he ordered Jay to pay the minimum of $311 per month.

A standard provision in Judge Lindemood's orders in the past had been what is referred to around here as the morality clause. Almost all of my prior orders in Judge Lindemood's Court contained a provision that both parents would be enjoined from "permitting an unrelated adult with whom the conservator has a romantic or dating relationship from remaining in the same residence as the children between the hours of 10:00 p.m. and 8:00 a.m."

We put that provision into the decree of divorce when we appeared for the judge to sign it on July 20, 2021 (the judge had verbally rendered the divorce on May 25, 2021). Jay and his lawyer objected and wanted the morality clause taken out. Judge Lindemood struck it out at their request, placing a big *X* across the wording. He then signed the decree of divorce.

Janice had her boys back (at least 56 percent of the time) and was free to move out of Midland County, Texas. On June 2, 2021,

Janice and her boys moved into an apartment in Odessa, Ector County, Texas.

PUZZLE PIECES

- Why do you think Judge Lindemood denied discovery regarding the fact that Jay was banned from being called as a substitute for MISD?
- Why do you think Jay was banned from teaching at MISD? Would that have been relevant information to have in the trial?
- What does removing the morality clause, a standard provision in his cases, signal about Judge Lindemood's interests in protecting the children from exposure to Jay's multiple sexual partners in this case, especially in light of the evidence of Jay's promiscuous hookups with men he met on Grindr?
- Why would Judge Lindemood give a father with this kind of conduct maximum visitation in this custody case?
- How do you feel about the judge ordering Jay to pay the bare minimum of child support and not covering Janice's attorney's fees?
- Based on what you've read thus far, do you see a pattern developing?
- Did you notice that Janice's jury trial began on May 17, 2021, the same date as Jack Marshall's article discussed in chapter 9, "On the Payroll"?

Chapter 15

NEW VENUE, NEW JUDGE

In 2022, nearly one in three victims of child sexual abuse substantiated by US child-welfare agencies were under the age of nine.[1]

The Texas Family Code is the statutory law passed by the Texas legislature that controls issues involving marriage, divorce, custody (conservatorship), visitation, child support, adoption, protective orders, termination of parental rights, and so forth. It also sets out the rules on which courts have jurisdiction and which counties have venue.

When a court order involving minor children is entered and final in Texas (e.g., a final decree of divorce), that court maintains jurisdiction over the children for hearing future modification and enforcement motions until they turn eighteen, are legally emancipated, or graduate from high school *unless* the case is transferred to another county on a motion to transfer venue.

The Texas Family Code states you can file such a motion if your children have lived in the new county for at least six months. At that point, the transfer is mandatory upon the filing of the proper motion to modify, along with the motion to transfer venue. If either party filed a motion to modify or motion for enforcement before meeting the six-month residency requirement, this action would reopen the case in the original court of continuing jurisdiction. In that instance, motions for modification, clarification, and enforcement would continue to be heard by the original court.

At the point Janice won the jury verdict and got custody of her sons back, it was the first time she had had them overnight for more than two nights per month for over fifteen months. Even with the revised custody, they still had to go with Jay for his weekend visits, *and* he got the whole month of July as the noncustodial parent pursuant to the standard possession order. Although she had just achieved an amazing victory in the courtroom before the jury, the judge set up Jay's visitation with more time than Janice during the first two months that the boys were back in her custody.

During the fifteen months that Jay had been named as temporary sole managing conservator, Janice had no rights to take the children to any counselors. Now that she had the full rights to take them to counseling, she had to be rather circumspect regarding this issue. She knew that if she took them to counseling and they made an outcry of sexual abuse or anything the counselor believed to be an act requiring a report to CPS or the police, she would end up back in Judge Lindemood's court again if it happened within the first six months after moving away from Midland.

Janice continued to see signs that her children were acting out sexually. She even received calls from their teacher informing her that one of her boys was masturbating in class. The after-school worker told Janice he was showing off in a "dirty dancing" manner. All kinds of red flags were being raised during the initial six-month period, indicating that her children needed counseling. As hard as it was for Janice, she had to hold off on taking them in for an appointment to get the care they needed, because she realized another hearing in front of Judge Lindemood would probably put them right back into the custody of Jay.

Once Janice had lived in Ector County for the six-month period, we decided to file for a modification of the terms of the divorce decree. First, we went after the lowball figure on the child support. She needed more than the bare minimum of $311 per month that had been set by Judge Lindemood. So we filed a motion requesting an increase in child support. By then, Jay was working as a realtor. Surely he was making more than minimum wage. We also asked for a restriction to get the morality clause added back into the order so that Jay couldn't allow his lovers and Grindr hookups to be around the boys at night.

We had learned the name of one of the men who Jay was bringing around the boys. Our research and investigation revealed that this man was under a protective order in Oklahoma and not allowed to come around his own children. In our motion to modify, we asked that Jay be enjoined from allowing this man around the boys at all. Along with our motion to modify, we filed a motion to transfer venue to Ector County.

Although it took a few days after filing the motions and obtaining service on Jay, the order transferring the case to Ector County was signed by Judge Lindemood, as this transfer was mandatory. Now the case would be heard by Judge Sara Kate Billingsley, the district judge in the 446th Judicial District Court in Ector County, Texas.

While the days passed for the district clerk of Midland County to get the file transferred to the district clerk of Ector County,

Janice made an appointment with Tommy Pool to get the boys back into counseling.

On February 16, 2022, the boys made statements to Pool that they had watched videos with Dad (Jay) in which men were naked and doing things to boys. They also told Tommy that Dad photographed them in the shower. Tommy reported these statements to CPS.

Upon hearing this, Lane Haygood and I filed an application for a protective order. The boys were interviewed by CPS worker Gordon Monyei, who set up a forensic interview at the Children's Advocacy Center in Midland. Radhika Gafur with the CAC confirmed that the children had made outcries consistent with what Tommy had reported. And she told us she believed the outcries were genuine.

On February 17, 2022, Judge Billingsley signed a temporary ex parte protective order, initially setting up a hearing on March 4, 2022. In turn, Jay hired Odessa attorney Gaven Norris. Due to scheduling conflicts, a bomb threat at the courthouse, and a flood in the courtroom causing the hearing to be reset repeatedly, we didn't begin the hearing for this protective order until April 13, 2022.

For that first hearing, we had issued subpoenas for the CPS worker, the woman conducting the forensic interview, Midland Police Detective David Olvera, schoolteachers, and the principal. When we called Detective Olvera to the stand, we learned that he had allowed one month to pass from the time the children made their outcry before he obtained the cell phone from Jay to copy the contents in a phone dump.

He testified he had examined the contents of Jay's phone and found no inappropriate photos of the children. In fact, he had already closed the case. Although we had subpoenaed Detective

Olvera to bring an exact copy of the phone dump on Jay's phone, he showed up in court without complying with our subpoena. Judge Billingsley stopped his testimony at that point and instructed the police officer that he had one hour to drive back to Midland, get the flash drive of the phone dump, and get it back to her courtroom in Odessa.

The judge did not appreciate the detective disregarding the subpoena. As soon as Detective Olvera returned with the flash drive containing the phone dump, it was entered into evidence. Although he testified under oath that this flash drive was a complete copy of everything on Jay's phone and that it was his only phone, nothing on the phone dump had anything regarding the Grindr app. In fact, it had very few pictures of the boys, although the testimony was that this was Jay's only phone and the same one he had had prior to the jury trial.

In all of my decades of trying contested custody trials, the one thing parents consistently have is a whole lot of pictures of their kids on their phone. Even though this phone dump was devoid of cute, fun pictures of Dad and the boys doing things together (remember: he had sole custody for fifteen months, so he had time to take lots of pictures of his sons), he had forty creepy pictures of the Devil and other types of evil-looking characters on his phone. When I questioned Jay at a later hearing about the creepy Devil pictures, he couldn't explain why they were on his phone. The phone dump also revealed text messages that were very significant to me.

The phone dump revealed that Jay had a very extensive text message dialogue with veteran CPS worker Olivia Quezada. She was the CPS worker who had come to Midland from her home base of El Paso when a report had been made against Jay regarding the elder son contracting molluscum contagiosum. Her findings and investigation came to a conclusion that "ruled out" any wrongdoing by Jay against the boys. Quezada testified at the jury trial. My experience over the years in dealing with CPS workers is that they keep their professional distance from the people they are investigating.

The jury verdict had come in on Friday, May 21, 2021, and all twelve jurors had voted unanimously in favor of Janice. Therefore, it was really surprising to me to see Jay and Quezada in a lengthy text message exchange with one another the day after the jury verdict was announced in open court on Saturday, May 22, 2021. After texting back and forth for several minutes, Jay texted the following to Quezada at 14:24:14:

> "From my understanding the Judge was as shocked as the rest of us."
>
> Quezada then texted back at 14:24:48:
>
> "I can imagine he was. He knows everything."

I was completely stunned. Where would Jay get any information that the judge was shocked? Who told Jay that? There were no comments on the record that Judge Lindemood was shocked by the ruling. There were no in-chambers conferences with all lawyers in attendance with the judge in which he told us he was shocked by the jury verdict.

Another text message exchange included in the phone dump on the day of the jury verdict (May 21, 2021) again indicated Jay had some inside information about Judge Lindemood's thoughts. This was a text message exchange between Jay and his friend Jon Ross Culbreath at 17:38:52:

"What did the judge say? I'm shocked!"

Jay replied at 17:39:20:

"He was shocked."

The phone dump revealed a text message exchange between Jay and his mother in January 2021, prior to the May jury trial. On January 5, 2021, at 19:31:31, Jay texted:

"And [Jacob] was [*sic*] the spots."

As it turned out, the "spots" were molluscum contagiosum, and now the younger child had contracted the condition. Seven minutes later, he texted his mother:

"I do not need this right now."

On January 26, 2021, Jay texted his mother that he had too much money in the bank. She texted back at 11:10:21:

"Need to put it in my name."

Again at 11:21:42, his mom texted him:

"I'm serious about putting it in my name."

All of the phone dump text messaging dialogue, as well as the demonic photos, came into evidence during the thirteen days (thus far) of trial on our application for a lifetime protective order. As of the writing of this chapter, we have volumes of evidence submitted and admitted before the judge to consider in making her decision and her ruling. We also have many hours of testimony from both parents and numerous witnesses. Each side has been given ample opportunity to present testimony and documents.

As of this writing, we have gone through thirteen days of trial spread out over almost two years. The ex parte protective order is still in place, prohibiting Jay from contacting or coming around the boys. We were in court on January 29, 2024, thinking we were down to the last two days of testimony and evidence. We were hoping to get a ruling granting a lifetime protective order by the end of the day on January 31, 2024, but the case was continued until May 15, 16, and 17, 2024. New evidence came in that Monday that would require additional time for the judge to read.

That evidence consisted of hundreds of pages of counseling records from the children's psychologist in Houston and a report that had come into the possession of Jay's attorney, Norris. The report admitted into evidence on January 29, 2024, appeared to be a homicide investigation in Blaine County, Oklahoma, prepared by the sheriff's office. It recited the children's remarks and statements on CAC interviews conducted in Odessa at the request of the Ector County Sheriff's Office and a CAC interview from Midland at the request of Homeland Security. I have many questions as to how and why Jay and his attorney are in possession of the homicide investigation report where Jay is the named suspect for murder.

This report states that the boys had talked about two murders committed by their dad on the property owned by Jay's parents. One victim was a girl named Joy; the other was a little boy named Josh. The following contains excerpts from the report.

On page 6 of 39, the report states:

On May 16, 2023, Investigator Heide Zavala from Ector County Sheriff's Office made contact with dispatch, who transferred the call to me. I, Investigator Joshua Wilder, spoke with Zavala about a disclosure two young boys had made in Odessa, Texas, regarding a possible murder of a juvenile female here in Blaine County, Oklahoma, near the city of Hydro. There were four victims, but the boys only knew the names of two, Joy, eight-year-old female and Joshua, a male. Joy was shot in the chest and thrown into a creek/lake, and Joshua was shot in the chest while tied to a rocking chair inside his grandparents home. Joshua was place [*sic*] into a compost pile and then removed from it and relocated somewhere else on the property. The kids called them "lumps" and there was supposed to be multiple "lumps" on the property.

On page 7 of 39, the report states:

Jacob explained "Joy" was and [*sic*] 8 year old girl who would climb over the fence to play with the boys. They would commonly play in the ditch on "Nana and Papa's" property. "Joy" was described as long brown hair with brown eyes wearing a white dress at the time she was murdered. Jacob said she was shot with a "sniper rifle" in the chest and thrown into the water. Jacob describes this area as the water next to the water fall. It should be noted based on the image from Google there is a large pond on the property which has an over flow spot that could look like a water fall where the pond is over flowing. Based on the google images this over flow runs into a creek which eventually runs into the North Canadian River.

Jacob describes the grandparent being home and knowing about the little girl being shot. Jacob goes on to say the grandparents tried to kill him and his brother with a gun at some point in the past.

Jacob says "Joy" was shot when they were last at the grandparents home when he was 6, he is now 8. This would put the last known child being shot around 2021 and I assume it would be around summer time since they were playing in the water. The boys were with their father for 15 months because custody was taken from Janice at the time.

Jacob also spoke a little of the case were [*sic*] his father had cut him and his brother and smeared it on the walls of the room they were in. He was asked how he was cut and he said on his arms and legs. He was also asked if he had marks from this and he said no he heals really fast due to him being accustomed to the abuse.

Joseph was the last interview I watched and the most disturbing. "Joshua" is the first child Joseph spoke of. From Joseph's account he was at his "Nana and Papa's" home and was woken up to someone crying. When he went into the living room, he sees a boy tied to a rocking chair. The [*sic*] gave him the name of "Joshua" and had brown hair and brown eyes. "Joshua" asked Joseph to call his mom for him and began to give the number when he was shot with a rifle by Jay. Jay then put "Joshua" into a compost for several days then relocated him to what Joseph calls "lumps." Joseph also state [*sic*] there are a lot of these lumps" on his grandparents property.

Joseph described the home were [*sic*] the murders took place as a gray metal building house with a red roof. The image he drew looked to be in the shape of an A. It should be noted Joseph's grandparents currant [*sic*] home has a red metal roof base [*sic*] on google images of the property.

In the interview I was made aware of possible 4 [*sic*] victims Joseph had witnessed be murdered at this home. He could only recall "Joshua's" name and said "Joy" told Jacob her name, but not him. Joseph was only willing to speak about two of the murders at the time of the interview.

"Joy" was murdered in a very similar fashion as "Joshua." She was reported be [*sic*] have been shot in a rocking chair in the home. Joseph described her as "almost blonde" with green eyes. "Joy" was then thrown into the "lake." Joseph said his grandparents watch [*sic*] this happen in the living room. It should be noted this incident does not match Jacobs. I am not sure if this is the same little girl or a different one.

Both of the incident[s] described by Joseph happened with a rifle. Like Jacob, Joseph was also threatened he would die just like them if he ever told.

On page 14 of 39 of the Blaine County Sheriff's report, it states:

On June 6th, 2023, at approximately 09:14 hours, I contacted OSBI agent Trevor Ridgeway via XXX. This was done because it is known to us that Agent Ridgeway is a personal friend of Jay's and is likely to garner his trust. I asked Agent Ridgeway if he would be willing to make a call to Jay and ask him if he would be willing to take a polygraph examination.

Agent Ridgeway stated that he was happy to make the call, but he advised me that Jay has since retained a Lawyer in this matter, and Lawyers almost never permit a polygraph. I presented an alternative to cooperate with the investigation by permitting us to run dogs trained in locating Cadavers on his parents property in Hydro. Investigator Ridgeway stated that he would present that idea to Jay as well . . . Agent Ridgeway advised me to call Jay directly as that may serve to help things along. At approximately 09:48 hours, I contacted Jay via XXX. I introduced myself as an Investigator of the Blaine County Sheriff's Office. I explained to Jay that I am not trying to get any information from him and that I understand he has retained a Lawyer. I explained to him that I would like to have cadaver dogs search his parents property in Hydro in an effort to find the truth. Jay stated that he would let his parents know of our intentions and would have them get back to us. At approximately 13:05 hours, "Jay's father" returned my call. I recorded the phone call with my Body Camera. "Jay's father" stated that he has spoken to his Lawyer and was advised to only allow the dogs on his property if they are certified through OSBI. "Jay's father" asked me where the dogs would be coming from, and I advised him that I became aware of the cadaver dogs through my Sherriff Travis Daugherty. I further advised "Jay's father" that the Dogs would be coming from an outside agency as we do not have dogs that are trained to locate Cadavers. "Jay's father" stated that if the Dogs were not State certified to contact his Lawyer XXX.

At approximately 13:10 hours, I contacted Sheriff Daugherty who explained to me that the Dogs would likely be coming from OSBI and that his contacts for the dogs have not returned his calls. At approximately 14:00 hours, I conducted another recorded phone call with "Jay's father" and explained to him that the Dogs would be coming from OSBI and that he would be notified when we are able to facilitate that. I advised "Jay's father" not to dig on his property in the mean time. "Jay's father" stated that he is not supposed to speak with me anymore and I agreed to contact his Lawyer going forward.

On page fifteen of thirty-nine of the report, it states:

On June 10, 2023 at approximately 08:46 hours, a consensual K9 search of the residence located at XXX in the City of Hydro, County of Blaine, State of Oklahoma was conducted. I had previously received written authorization from the property owners lawyer XXX. I presented a Permission to Search form to the property owner "Jay's father" and he signed it in my presence. Three K9 handlers were provided to us by K9 Search OK INC. They were Becky McKinney, Molly Gibb, and Sydney Rubin. The K9's used were trained in locating human remains. An extensive search of the area was conducted with the K9's that lasted approximately four and half hours. Blaine County Investigators David Duggan and Josh Wilder were present as well as Sheriff Travis Daugherty and myself. There were two areas of interest that K9's alerted to. A large pile of dirt located to the south east of the residence just to the north of the large waterfall and a small pond to the south west of the property right by the main road. It should be noted that the aforementioned pond does not exist

> throughout the year and was only there due to recent rainfall. This was confirmed via our previous photographs of the property. Because the pond was not always present and the area in question is in full view of the neighbors, we focused our efforts on the dirt pile. "Jay's father" agreed to help us excavate the loose dirt with his tractor. At approximately 13:45 hours, we began to excavate the earth approximately a foot or two at a time. Each time a bucket of earth was removed Investigator Duggan would sift through the dirt. The dirt pile itself was also dug through with shovels by Investigator Wilder and I. At approximately 14:31 hours, our search of the dirt pile was concluded and no human remains were found . . .

On pages thirty-one and thirty-two of thirty-nine, the May 16, 2023, CAC interview was typed out regarding the interview by Ector County Investigator Heidi Zavala and Joseph, the elder child. (Remember that I am continuing to use different names for the purpose of this book for Janice, my client; Jay, her ex-husband; Joseph, their elder child; and Jacob, their younger child, rather than their actual names.)

Investigator: You were telling her about a little boy named Joshua? I couldn't hear you, so I had to come visit with you. OK, so was this little boy like your age?

Joseph: Almost my age.

Investigator: Almost your age. So, he was a little bit smaller than you. So, was he like 7 when all this happened?

Joseph: No, he was like 5.

Investigator: He was like 5? And you don't know where he came from? Was he like a neighbor?

Joseph: I don't know where he came from.

Investigator: And he had brown hair and brown eyes, you said. OK. And this is when you were about 6 or 7? (Joseph nods affirmative.) When you guys were in Weatherford? (Joseph shook his head yes.) Where [*sic*] you all living in Weatherford?

Joseph: No, we were living in? [*sic*] Oklahoma.

Investigator: Right. You were staying with your grandparents.

Joseph: No, we were staying with my Nana and Papa.

Investigator: So you were staying with your Nana and Papa. Did this little boy come over to stay the night? Did Joshua come over to stay the night? (Joseph shakes his head no.) No, cause he wasn't there right before you went to bed. But you woke up the next morning and you heard him crying. Right. Where was he crying out again?

Joseph: In the living room.

Investigator: In the living room. Was there anything on TV or anything?

Joseph: No.

Investigator: No. So he was just crying. Did he tell you why he was crying?

Joseph: Um, he was telling me his number, but before he could tell me it. His mom's phone number. he [*sic*] came in, My [*sic*] dad came in and shot him before he could tell me.

Investigator: like [*sic*] there in the living room? Where were you sitting when that happened?

Joseph: I just got out of bed so I was just standing there and I came out and saw he was crying so I went over to him he [*sic*] was going to tell me his name, Joshua, and his phone number, but before he could my dad shot him.

Investigator: Do you remember what the gun looked like your dad shot him with?

Joseph: (Shook his head.) No.

Investigator: No? Do you remember? So, was he sitting on the couch when your dad shot him?

Joseph: No, he was in the chair.

Investigator: What kind of chair was it?

Joseph: Was a, you know, a kind of chair that you rocked back and forth in.

Investigator: Like a rocking chair.

Joseph: And he was tied.

Investigator: Oh. What was he tied with?

Joseph: rope or something

Investigator: You said it was in a metal building. Was it like a . . .

Joseph: It was like a house. An all-metal house.

Investigator: So it was like a barn kind of house. Was this on your grandparents' property?

Joseph: yes.

Investigator: So it was a metal barn kind of house. Is this where your dad would stay?

Joseph: yes (inaudible 3:38).

Investigator: So your dad shot little Joshua in the rocking chair? what color was the chair

Joseph: It was a normal wood color.

Investigator: Was it brown? And then after he shot him, what happened?

Joseph: He threw him into the compost. And then they let him sit set a couple of days. But then they dug out the things that were holding it together. So now it's in the dirt. But there's a lot of worms in there, at my nana and papa.

Investigator: So they just buried little Joshua? Who did they throw in the lake?

Joseph: who?

Investigator: Yeah. Did they throw somebody in the lake?

Joseph: Yeah.

Investigator: Who got thrown in the lake?

Joseph: It was a little girl. But my brother knows her name.

Investigator: Were you there when that happened?

Joseph: yes, me and my brother were there.

Investigator: And how old were you when that one happened?

Joseph: Still 6 and my brother was still 5.

Investigator: Oh, okay. What was this little girl's name?

Joseph: I don't know it.

Investigator: You don't have to remember her name.

Joseph: She didn't tell me her name, she only told my brother.

Investigator: oh, okay. So, what happened with that?

Joseph: she got shot and he threw her to the lake and she had like blonde, almost blonde hair and light green . . .

Without going into details of the multiple pages of evidence and testimony during these thirteen days of trial, I will say that it contains the most troubling facts of any case in my four and a half decades as a lawyer. The children reported being sexually abused by their dad and multiple other men. They also stated they had been sold, caged, ritualistically abused, photographed and filmed in sexual acts, trafficked, transported, and flown to places in Texas, Oklahoma, and elsewhere. And they have witnessed multiple murders of children and adults and can describe in detail what happened to the bodies of those killed (buried, burned, thrown in the river, etc.). Joseph was hospitalized for a period of time for wanting to kill himself, and he made additional detailed outcries.

Homeland Security began an investigation in August 2022, meeting with Janice multiple times. After they conducted a CAC forensic interview of the children in September 2022 and a SANE (Sexual Assault Nurse Examiner) Exam at Midland Memorial Hospital, a search warrant was served on Jay, and fifteen to twenty agents were at his apartment for several hours on October 25, 2022, seizing multiple electronic devices. We do not know the current status of their investigation, and we have not received any notice that it has been closed. Nevertheless, Jay's attorney had to turn over the report from Blaine County, Oklahoma, in his possession, and it was admitted into evidence for the judge in our case to review. This Blaine County sheriff's report contains details about the Homeland Security investigation.

As of this writing, Janice's case remains open. We were last in court May 15–17, 2024. At that hearing, an exceedingly disturbing document was admitted into evidence. We have been advised that this piece of evidence is under investigation by the FBI. I personally hand delivered the document to the new Midland County district attorney, Glenn Harwood, on June 12, 2025. Throughout the trial, Jay has testified under oath that everything the boys have said is a lie.

PUZZLE PIECES

- Does it concern you that Detective Olvera waited an entire month to obtain and copy the contents in Jay's phone?
- As you read this chapter, how many of these people do you think were acting with ignorance, incompetence, or alliance with "The Club"?
- Does it concern you there were almost no pictures of Jay's children and no Grindr app on the dump of Jay's phone, even though he had a presence on Grindr and was the sole custodian of the boys for fifteen months?
- Why do you think Jay had Devil pictures on his phone?
- Do you find it significant that Jay's texts suggested he had inside knowledge of the judge's reaction to a jury verdict?

Chapter 16

THE PROBLEM WITH CHILD PROTECTIVE SERVICES

In the United States, about 70 percent of child-maltreatment reports to Child Protective Services (CPS) come from professionals such as teachers, medical staff, and law enforcement—yet fewer than one in five reports are substantiated after investigation.[1]

In this book, I have made references to Child Protective Services, an agency in the state of Texas commonly called CPS. Officially, it is named the Texas Department of Family and Protective Services (DFPS). In the four-plus decades of my legal career, I've had CPS workers and investigators involved in my clients' cases from time to time. Sometimes it was my client being the one investigated or accused of abuse or neglect, and sometimes it was my client's spouse or ex-spouse being investigated.

I do not claim to be an expert on CPS cases, but I have dealt with enough of them to have acquired experience and formed my own observations and opinions. Many people who have dealt with CPS in Texas for any length of time come to the conclusion that it is an agency that is deeply flawed and plagued by systemic deficiencies that work against the welfare of the children. This conclusion was clearly set out in Federal Judge Janis Graham Jack's opinion on December 17, 2015, when she entered a scathing memorandum opinion and verdict of the court against CPS and various people in administrative positions within the agency. The lawsuit was styled M.D.; bnf Stukenberg, et al., Plaintiffs, vs. Greg Abbott, et al., Defendants, in the United States District Court, Southern District Court of Texas, Corpus Christi Division, Civil Action No. 2:11-CV-84.

The opinion starts by saying the following:

> Plaintiffs brought this class action under 42 U.S.C. §1983 against officials of the State of Texas. Plaintiffs Claim that Texas Violates their Fourteenth Amendment substantive due process rights, including "the right to be reasonably safe from harm while in government custody and the right to receive the most appropriate care, treatment, and services" by how the State and its officials manage the Department of Family and Protective Services and the departments under its control.

The opinion continues, stating the following:

> Texas's foster care system has a checkered history. In 2009, the Texas Legislature and Governor Perry formed the Texas Adoption Review Committee 'to take a hard look at the Texas foster care system.' The Committee conducted a ten-month review, which included testimony from DFPS employees, foster care advocates, policy analysts, foster and adoptive parents, CPAs, and experts from ten areas of DFPS.

> *Id.* at 8. The Committee reviewed articles, reports, and publications, including one by the Child Welfare League of America ("CWLA"), one by Specia (not yet DFPS Commissioner), and a report by Texas Appleseed that had previously been submitted to the Texas Supreme Court Commission for Children, Youth, And Families. *Id.* at 25–28. After drafting its recommendations, the 2009 Committee unearthed a report from 1996, produced by a similarly charged committee that was formed by Governor George W. Bush. *Id.* at 2, 7. The 2009 Committee found that 11 of its 14 general recommendations were made in 1996, leading it to conclude that "many of the same problems identified in 1996" had not been fixed. *Id.* at 2, 7-12. The Committee released its final report in December 2010. At the outset the report notes that, despite the good intentions and hard work of the people involved in Texas's child welfare system, "there is increasing evidence to show that our foster care system is sometimes *doing more harm* to our children than good." *Id.* at 2.

This lawsuit had to do with a vast array of children under the care of CPS in the foster care division of the agency. The description of abuse, negligence, and malfeasance inflicted upon the children in Texas who were turned over to the care of CPS—the workers, caretakers, and placement facilities—was beyond sad and regrettable. It was shocking and sometimes horrific. The children in this lawsuit were not identified by their actual names but by their initials because they were minors. The 260-page judgment went on and on describing the abuses and neglect inflicted upon these Texas children.

In the conclusions of the opinion, Judge Jack states the following:

> Texas's foster care system is broken, and it has been that way for decades. It is broken for all stakeholders, including DFPS employees who are tasked with impossible workloads. Most importantly, though, it is broken for Texas's PMC children, who almost uniformly leave State custody more damaged than when they entered.
>
> The Court believes that Specia and his staff have the best intentions to run an effective foster care system. The Court is also mindful that Specia is the seventh commissioner since 2004, each of whom was surely ushered in with promises that this time it will be different. The reality is that DFPS has ignored 20 years' of reports, outlining problems and recommending solutions. DFPS has also ignored professional standards. All the while, Texas's PMC children have been shuttled throughout a system where rape, abuse, psychotropic medication, and instability are the norm. The Court has no assurance that anything has changed. Of the two reforms to which DFPS pointed—CPS Transformation and Foster Care Redesign—one was instituted in the wake of this lawsuit, the other is an abject failure, and neither answers any of Plaintiff's claims.
>
> Plaintiffs have a Fourteenth Amendment substantive due process right to be free from an unreasonable risk of harm caused by the State. Texas currently violates that right.

SIGNED and ORDERED this 17th day of December, 2015.

—Janis Graham Jack

Senior United States District Judge

I urge you to take a moment and think about what this federal judge's opinion is describing. The very agency in Texas that is supposed to be helping and caring for these children is causing them extreme harm. Judge Jack said so in her findings. How could such abuse and negligence exist within the very agency that is supposed to protect children who are at greatest risk? Why were these children in the foster care system in the first place? Maybe one or both of the parents were deceased, in prison, or suffered from drug addiction or mental illness. Maybe the parent(s) had been abusive and had their rights terminated. Certainly, you get the picture, but when the agency personnel provide homes and placements that are as bad as or worse than the ones they were removed from, then we really have placed these children into a life directed toward misery and tragedy.

This chapter is not written to be an exposé on Judge Jack's opinion, the systemic problems with CPS, the foster care system in Texas, or the efforts to clean it up. I am telling you about Judge Jack's judgment to point out the decades of failure and abuse doled out by the Texas Department of Family and Protective Services.

My dealings with CPS have not been about the foster care system but rather the investigative aspect of the CPS system, in which a caseworker shows up when a complaint or call is made that a child has been abused or neglected, or the caller has reason to believe there has been abuse or neglect.

The Texas Family Code in Section 261.101 says, "A person having reasonable cause to believe that a child's physical or mental health or welfare has been adversely affected by abuse or neglect by any person *shall* immediately make a report as provided by this sub chapter." This section goes on to describe that people working in certain professions and occupations are considered mandatory reporters if abuse or neglect of a child is known or suspected. These are people who work in medicine, education, mental health counseling and therapy, law, and ministry, just to name a few. Someone who is working in one of these areas who becomes aware that a child has been abused or neglected and fails to report it to CPS or law enforcement is subject to arrest and criminal charges being brought for failure to report. The Texas Family Code states that the report must be made no later than the forty-eighth hour after the professional first has reasonable cause to believe that the child has been or may have been abused or neglected. It is also a crime to make a false report to CPS or to law enforcement.[2]

Typically, when CPS is involved in one of my cases and I issue a subpoena to CPS for the caseworker to bring the full report to a hearing or a deposition, someone within CPS takes the time to redact the name of the person who made the initial report. They also take out other things in the report they consider confidential. Sometimes, it takes weeks, or even months, to find out what is in the report, and even then, what we receive is incomplete, given all the redactions.

It has been my observation that there are sometimes people who make false reports and allegations to the police and to CPS. Sometimes, it is because the parties are involved in a divorce or custody battle, and one parent is trying to gain an advantage over the other by making false allegations. Other times, a parent is, in fact, abusing a child, and the good parent learns about it and reports it to CPS. It would naturally follow that the good parent would file for divorce against the abusive parent and the good parent would ask for custody and restrictions on access and possession of the child against the abuser.

It confounds me to hear such ignorant words coming from some

CPS caseworker who says at the very beginning of an investigation something along the lines of "Well, this parent is just trying to gain an advantage in a custody dispute" or "I only see this kind of allegation in a divorce or custody dispute, so it must be made up."

When I hear statements like these, I always counter with something along the lines of "Do you think a parent who just learned that the other parent has abused their child should *not* file for divorce? Do you think the parent should *not* start a custody suit?"

Of course, these kinds of facts go hand in hand with lawsuits for divorce and custody. Of course, there are some mean, vindictive parents who fabricate false allegations and false charges. There are also truthful, courageous parents who report abuse and neglect. There are laws that require mandatory reporters to notify the law enforcement authorities and CPS when they see or learn of evidence of abuse or neglect. And it is the responsibility of CPS caseworkers and law enforcement to do a genuine and thorough investigation regarding the facts of each case.

My cases are divorce and custody cases, so when the facts and allegations are in the nature of abuse or neglect, that is when CPS becomes involved. Not all custody disputes rise to the level of abuse or neglect. Many times, the two parents are in disagreement over parenting style, discipline, medical decisions, educational decisions, or extracurricular activities. Early in my career, I tried a jury trial in which the biggest issue in the dispute was how and when the potty training for a little boy was to be conducted. In my experience, CPS rarely gets involved in my clients' cases. However, if the facts are such that true abuse and/or neglect is apparent, the law *requires* that we report it to CPS.

At the time I began representing Janice in June 2020, there

had already been two CPS reports and investigations. A third CPS report was made two or three months after I signed a contract to begin representing her. This third report involved Olivia Quezada, the veteran CPS worker from El Paso, who traveled from El Paso to investigate a report on the condition of molluscum contagiosum bumps on the older boy's genital area. She ruled out any allegations that this could have been caused by sexual abuse while in Dad's care even though the child had contracted the condition while he was exclusively in the possession of Dad and it was during the COVID-19 lockdown. This veteran CPS worker had zero concerns that Dad or any of the people he was allowing around the boys might be abusing the child.

Little did we know that around August and September 2020, when she began "investigating" these allegations, she was becoming so aligned with Jay that her communications with him continued even after she had cleared him of any abuse allegations. In fact, Olivia Quezada and Jay were texting each other twenty-four hours after the jury verdict came in on May 22, 2021. It appeared they had become friendly enough that she was on his side regarding the outcome of the jury trial. Remember the string of text messages we saw as a result of the phone dump of Jay's phone in February 2022? Olivia Quezada wanted to know from Jay what the judge thought about the jury totally reversing Judge David Lindemood's prior temporary ruling naming Jay as the sole managing conservator. Why would she even expect that Jay could answer the question as to what the judge thought after twelve jurors had heard a full week of testimony and evidence regarding Jay and Janice and their children? Why did Olivia Quezada carry on dialogue with him in such a friendly and partial manner? Why was she communicating with him at all? Everything about CPS worker Quezada and her investigation, her ruling, and her private communications with Jay raised more questions than answers.

When Tommy Pool made his mandatory report to CPS in February 2022, this event put into action the series of filings, orders, and hearings that bring us to the ex parte protective order signed by Judge Sara Kate Billingsley under which we continue to operate as of October 14, 2025. You may also remember CPS worker Gordon Monyei, whose investigation was conducted after the outcry by Janice's two boys, which caused Mr. Pool to make his mandatory report.

On May 18, 2022, Mr. Monyei issued a letter stating there was *Reason to Believe* that Jay had committed sexual abuse on both boys. It is very important to note that this is the *only* time that any CPS worker has issued any letter or finding that Jay has committed any sexual abuse on either child.

On November 9, 2022, a CPS worker named Lisa M. Flash, Investigator VI,* out of Abilene, Texas, signed off on a letter stating she had conducted an administrative review of investigative findings. She had, in essence, conducted a hearing in which Jay and his lawyer appealed the Monyei finding of *Reason to Believe* from May 18, 2022. Her letter and ruling totally reversed the Monyei findings, and now based upon her new ruling, the current disposition against Jay regarding the two boys is the following:

----

* Lisa M. Flash has signed her name as each of the following: Lisa M. Flash, Investigator VI; Lisa M. Flash, Protective Services for Family and Children; Lisa M. Flash, Appeals Resolution Specialist.

Ruled out for Sexual Abuse of Jacob
Ruled out for Sexual Abuse of Joseph

Flash had conducted a video Zoom hearing on Jay's appeal of the Monyei findings without ever notifying Janice or her attorneys, which is in violation of the Texas Administrative Code. Janice, Lane Haygood, and I were never notified of the appeal or that an administrative hearing was even taking place. According to their own CPS regulations, a requester (Jay) is eligible for an administrative review of investigative findings (ARIF) hearing only if a court has not made a previous finding against the requester consistent with the specific allegation for which he is requesting the ARIF (which it had). This type of finding includes that a court order specifically has found that the requester committed abuse or neglect in the situation for which he or she requested the ARIF (which it did).[3]

As I read the rules, Flash should never have conducted this hearing since Judge Billingsley had already signed her initial ex parte protective order making a finding that Jay had committed family violence. We had already had several hours and days of hearings before Judge Billingsley, with the children continuing to be protected by the ex parte protective order signed on February 17, 2022. And then along comes Flash in September 2022, and she conducts a hearing against the agency's own rules and reverses the *Reason to Believe* findings of Mr. Monyei, even while Judge Billingsley's temporary ex parte protective order and findings were still in place and while Homeland Security had begun an investigation.

When Flash was subpoenaed and appeared in court to testify before Judge Billingsley on April 5, 2023, she testified she had spent hours studying her file consisting of 1,378 pages. These pages contained her CPS records, showing a multitude of reports filed by mandatory reporters and those documents provided by Jay and his lawyer, Gaven Norris. Our legal team had analyzed these 1,378 pages, which included multiple copies of the divorce decree, copies of prior CPS records, and multiple copies of the first amended Petition to Modify (for child support). The packet was also loaded with totally irrelevant documents, such as kindergarten records on the younger child, an acknowledgment of electronic distribution of the student handbook for Midland Independent School District for April 2020, a special programs questionnaire for MISD for April 2020, and a media release parental consent form for MISD for April 2020.

In other words, Flash provided records as her "proof" that neither of these children had been sexually abused by filling up her 1,300-plus-page package with stuff that was irrelevant to the issue and pumped up by having multiple copies of other background documents. What she did *not* have were the forensic interviews of the children at the Children's Advocacy Center (CAC) conducted by Radhika Gafur in February 2022, where the children made their outcries of sexual abuse on video. Not only had Flash not watched these interviews, but she said she couldn't find them. As she testified, Flash probably did not know that I had watched the CAC interviews of the children conducted by Ms. Gafur and so had Gaven Norris, the lawyer for Jay.

The DVDs of the interviews had been made available to us to watch in the judge's office under the supervision of the judge's court reporter. Even more importantly, Judge Billingsley had advised us that she had watched these interviews. Flash also stated she did not have the CAC interviews of the children conducted at the request of the Homeland Security investigation of the children making the outcries. These Homeland Security interviews were totally separate from the ones conducted by Monyei and Gafur.

Yet with this ridiculously puffed-up packet of duplicates and irrelevant documents, this CPS Investigator VI conducted a one-sided review hearing that she should never have conducted and then wrote a letter stating *Ruled Out* for Jay to pass around to anyone and everyone he chooses to let them know he has been cleared of all allegations against him regarding sexually abusing his children. It is signed by Flash, and the letter bears the seal of Texas Department of Family and Protective Services.

We introduced an exhibit at the April 5, 2023, hearing on the day Flash testified before Judge Billingsley. This exhibit is a chart setting out the CPS reports that were made by various mandatory reporters regarding these two little boys. During the eleven months between May 18, 2022, when Monyei issued his *Reason to Believe* letter, and our April 5, 2023, hearing, there were fifteen additional reports of abuse against the father made by various individuals including counselors, medical and hospital personnel, and a school counselor.

Flash didn't have an explanation as to why she failed to rule *Unable to Determine*, which was one of her options. Instead, she readily signed her name on a letter, on official letterhead, stating that all allegations against Jay had been ruled out as of November 9, 2022. Since she did not state in her letter that she was specifically ruling out the Monyei findings of May 18, 2022, any person reading Flash's letter would be led to believe that Flash was ruling out all of the multiple CPS complaints against Jay leading up to November 9, 2022, including the reports as a result of the Homeland Security forensic interviews and the reports to Midland and Odessa Police Departments.

When I asked Flash on the witness stand why she even conducted the administrative review hearing in violation of their own rules and regulations, she stated, under oath, that a supervisor named Cynthia Asbury told her to do it. The testimony of this CPS "expert" left more unanswered questions and serious doubts as to CPS's ability to protect these two little boys.

After the November 9, 2022 (Flash), letter was issued, the May 18, 2022, *Reason to Believe* letter with findings by Monyei was changed as a result of the Flash ruling so that it now reads *Ruled Out*. To my knowledge, there are now no CPS findings by any CPS worker or CPS employee in the state of Texas that these two boys have been sexually abused by their father or while in his care. These findings and rulings fail to mention the ex parte protective order signed by Judge Billingsley, which is still in place as of this writing.

The November 9, 2022, letter by Flash wiped out and altered the findings of Monyei. Anyone who goes to CPS to learn the status of their findings regarding numerous reports filed against Jay on the subject of his abusive behavior toward his sons will only see a letter marked *Ruled Out*.

PUZZLE PIECES

- In your opinion, do the facts in this chapter show evidence of The Club at work?
- Why would CPS worker Olivia Quezada be on such friendly terms with a father accused of sexually molesting his children? And what is her connection to Judge Lindemood?
- Was Lisa Flash really unable to find the interviews?

- Does this chapter show you how deep and extensive the reach of The Club is? Or is this just a lone example of arrogance and incompetence while violating the policies and rules of the Texas Department of Family and Protective Services?
- Why are these CPS workers friendly with and ruling in favor of the father who is under a protective order and cannot see or come around his children and also has all of the creepy Devil pictures on his phone?

Chapter 17

LISTEN TO THE CHILDREN

More than 70 percent of victims who experience child sexual abuse wait five years or more before disclosing.[1]

In all of the years I have practiced law, I have represented mothers, fathers, grandparents, aunts, uncles, and siblings in regard to custody cases involving minor children. I have not represented the children themselves. There are lawyers who are court appointed by judges to represent and advocate for the children. Those lawyers carry the title *attorney ad litem* or *amicus attorney*. These lawyers have very specific duties and responsibilities to their clients (the children) and to the court. As a general rule, lawyers with these titles split the fee for their services equally between the mother and the father. These lawyers spend time with their client, talk to their client, and participate in the litigation from the perspective of the child.

As a lawyer hired by Mom and Dad, I do not typically visit with the minor child, even if there is no amicus attorney or attorney ad litem appointed to represent the child. It is frowned upon by the court for an attorney representing one of the parents in contested custody litigation to question the child or even visit with the child about their preferences. The rules in the Texas Family Code state that if a child of age twelve or older wants to state a preference as to where they want to live, a motion to confer is filed, and the child is to be interviewed by the judge in chambers. Sometimes, the judge will permit the parents' lawyers to be present during the interview, and sometimes, the interview is only the judge and the court reporter. Sometimes, the judge will ask the child to express reasons for wanting to live with Mom or with Dad. The judge still has complete discretion in deciding who will be the primary custodian, where the child will live, and what the visitation will be.

The subject matter of this book is not about the nuances of custody battles in Texas courts and where children want to live when they turn twelve or older. I have written about cases involving the sexual abuse and sex trafficking of children. These cases involve far more complicated issues than most lawyers and judges are prepared to recognize, understand, and deal with.

The fact that I have been consciously learning about this dark side of humanity for the last thirty years is in itself a slowly unfolding revelation. I have learned about child sex trafficking and the organized criminal aspect of this horrific abuse through the children's statements to CPS workers, counselors, medical doctors and nurses, forensic interviews, law enforcement, teachers, church personnel, and the parents.

These children are constantly telling others, or trying to tell others, what is going on through their drawings, their acting out, or their meltdowns, because they have been triggered by something that reminds them of some event or act of abuse that was inflicted upon them. If the child reaches the point of feeling safe enough with a counselor to begin describing their fears and what happened, it may be through play therapy or some other means of a skilled and trained psychologist that the truth begins to emerge.

I have learned from reading the hundreds, and into the thousands, of pages of counseling notes and CAC interviews that these children are not going to be forthcoming with the full extent of the abuse just because someone takes them into a twenty-minute or even two-hour forensic interview.

If this child has been sex trafficked, they have not only been sexually abused multiple times but almost certainly threatened against telling. The threats are terrifying. The perpetrators will threaten to kill them, their family, and anyone close to them. These threats are further amplified and sealed by the child whenever animals or other human beings are tortured or killed. In these cases, the abuser then tells them the same will happen to them if they tell. These children are not only physically injured or abused but also mentally and emotionally injured and abused. Just getting them away from the abuser does not mean that these children are okay. They need skilled, professional help, and they will need it for years to come.

On May 17, 2024, psychologist Dr. Hanh Vo, who at that time had been working with Janice's two sons over the past year, testified by Zoom in Janice's case. Excerpts from this testimony are as follows:

The Court: What is unique about working with children, who have been victims of sex-trafficking?

The Witness [Dr. Vo]: Children that has [*sic*] been, um, hurt and abused in general, they will have post-traumatic stress. Children with sex-trafficking, you're talking about multiple layers of trauma. There is the betrayal, there is the abandonment, there is the severe robbed [*sic*] and raped of their humanity, so they would have what is called complex PTSD [*sic*].

The Court: How do you diagnose or otherwise confirm that you are dealing with a child who has suffered sex-trafficking or something like it?

The Witness: There are very specific behaviors that manifested [*sic*] in kids that have been hurt by multiple adults.

The Court: Is it common for children, who are victims of sex-trafficking, to engage in an escalating pattern of revelations regarding abuse or outcries?

The Witness: Absolutely, absolutely, because the unraveling process have [*sic*] to be parallel with the process of reestablishing, rebuilding trust to an authority figure that the child can trust.

The Court: At what stage do you expect the outcries to increase in frequent [*sic*] and detail?

The Witness: Trust, yes, the more trust, the more safety, the more security, the more of the exploratory play the child is allowed in a safe and therapeutic environment, then the more the child is going to be able to come out.

Now, if the child is in a chronic stage of trauma, then the child is not going to be readily giving out information, because it would be more traumatizing and more of a safety issue for the child, so the child can only disclose and unravel abuse information in a safe environment, with trusting people, so their home have [*sic*] to be safe, their school have [*sic*] to be safe, their environment have [*sic*] to be safe in order for them to start coming out. The process may take years for that to happen.

The Court: What prompts the greater degrees of revelation? And, I think we're still speaking about children who are victims of sex-trafficking to—that engage in this escalating pattern of revelations, what—prompts the greater degrees of those revelations?

The Witness: It would be threefold. So, No. 1 is trust and safety, that ingredient, that foundation have [*sic*] to be established first, foremost, for any kind of self-disclosure or any kind of very, very deep-rooted, traumatic issues to come out, so safety and trust is one.

The second one would be triggering factors, things in the environment can trigger the child. Now, if the child is being triggered, but doesn't have a safety [*sic*] environment to reveal that, then the child is going to swallow the triggering, and it's going to turn into psychosomatic behaviors, so it's going to come out in a form of behavior versus verbally, vocally.

The third layers [*sic*] of for disclosing of abuse information from the child is the developmental aspect, the socio-emotional development of the child.

An example would be if the child was hurt pre-verbally, you know, the child doesn't have the vocabulary to tell you what happened to him or her, so you might have to wait until the child is a little bit older at school age, then the child is safe, the child would trigger, now the child has the vocabulary to tell you what happened.

But still, the child is not going to lucidly sit down and say, well, let me tell you what happened to me. It's going to come out in the form of play, art, it come [*sic*] out in a form of the child talking to himself, while he's doing the play.

So sometimes the child will say something that is completely disconnected from the environment. They are [*sic*] unrelated to what the child was doing. The information just popped out. It's like you hear the squeaking noise in the engine.

The Court: What emotional or mental triggers might children encounter that would prompt a disclosure of new facts?

The Witness: Fear, fear and terror, they immediately set them back to the fight and flight. So fight, flight, froze [*sic*] as part of our hard-wired self-preservation. That's the only part of us that was born completely formed, and the most sophisticated part of self-evolution.

Now, if the child doesn't have the vocabulary to tell you, then the child—when the child go into terror [*sic*], something triggering in the environment, it's going to activate the system, then the child is going to act out. So that's what society would be calling acting out. We call it just the fight and flight. It's just a very animalistic way of showing that the terror, the fear, have [*sic*] to be discharged somewhere.

The Court: How, in your therapeutic practice, do you handle internally inconsistent or contradictory narratives or revelations from the children?

The Witness: As treatment providers, there is no such thing as contradictory or inconsistent information. I understand that, because I understand the child process, healing is never a linear process, it's circular, child [*sic*] go back and forth, based on what's going on in the child's environment.

So child [*sic*] may feel safe one day in the environment, with fully nourishing, loving caregivers in the environment. Well, the next day the caregiver may go away, and the child is out of touch with that loving, home base, then the child immediately become [*sic*] more vulnerable, and feel [*sic*] more adrenaline, more cortisol pumping, more fight and flight, so the child become [*sic*] much more easily triggered when they're in a vulnerable environment.

The Court: What treatment options are available to reduce the triggering effect of events upon the children, who are victims of sex-trafficking and sexual abuse, and how does the Court support those efforts?

The Witness: No. 1, stop the abuse. Stop the endangerment of the child. Stop putting the child in harm's way.

So when a child say [*sic*], I know where the gun is, I'm going to go and take that gun, I'm going to shoot the perpetrator, we need to listen. What part of that, that we don't understand? What part of that is the mystery to us as a human race? Children don't make-up things like that, and they don't know—regular, unhurt, unharmed children would never say, I'm going to take my dad's gun, and I'm going to shoot him, I'm going to shoot myself.

If there is no evidence to support the claim of abuse, the evidence are [*sic*] in the children's socio-emotional behaviors. So children, again, they don't act out for no reason. They don't go to school and masturbate in front of the class. They

> don't refuse to use toilet paper because they were forced to eat toilet paper that was wiped by their caregiver. And these kind of stories are too meticulous and too outlandish to be falsified information to saw [*sic*] it on the TV or to hear somebody say it.
>
> When it is consistent information come [*sic*] out, and it's co—um, it's dysregulated the children's behaviors, it's tremendously impacted them. Children can make-up any kind of story. We know that children have a beautiful mind. They are highly imaginary creatures, but they cannot fake the emotion.

Following is an exhibit that was admitted into evidence in Janice's case from Dr. Hanh Vo, who provided expert testimony in her case. These suggestions come from her therapy notes. I believe this is very sound and helpful advice for any parent who is dealing with a child who has been abused, and I wanted to share it with you here.

IN EVERYDAY LIFE

- Establish regular routines for mealtimes, bedtimes, and school.
- Take notice of any changes in your child's behavior—for example, eating or sleeping differently or avoiding activities or places they used to enjoy.
- Share meals together regularly as a family. Talk about the things you'd normally talk about, like what people have been doing during the day.

- Spend time together as a family and with people your child likes and trusts. For example, play family board games, go for walks, watch TV together, and so on.
- Make time to talk with your child one to one—for example, while you're reading a book together before bed or driving to a sports game.
- Help your child to set small, achievable goals—for example, trying a new hobby or going to sports training every week.
- Praise your child's progress and improvements in all aspects of their life.

RELATIONSHIPS AND FEELINGS

- Tell your child that you love them and will always be there for them, no matter what.
- Show affection in the way that your child prefers. For example, your child might prefer a high five or fist bump rather than a hug or kiss.
- Be patient if your child seems angry or frustrated. When your child is sad, distressed, or worried, comfort and reassure them. Let them know their feelings are OK.
- Encourage your child to talk about their emotions and then label them together. You could say, "How are you feeling this morning? You're smiling—it looks like you're feeling happy."
- Use "feelings" pictures, posters, cards, or toys to help your child understand and express their feelings. Books about feelings can also help.

- This child is old enough to keep a diary or journal. Sometimes it's easier to write down or draw them than say them aloud.
- If your child has trouble talking about feelings, they might find it easier if you ask them how someone else might feel in this situation.

TALKING AND LISTENING

- Give your child space, time, and opportunities to talk about what has happened.
- Let your child know that you're there to listen and talk about anything whenever your child is ready. Nothing is so awful that your child can't talk about it with you.
- Actively listen to your child's concerns and feelings.
- Talk about being safe, feeling safe and having the right to feel safe. For example, you could talk about people your child can go to for help if they feel unsafe.
- Talk about sharing information about the sexual abuse.
- There will be good and not-so-good days. Keep giving your child as much support as you can, even on the not-so-good days. If you're not sure how to support your child, check in with the professional working with your child. Together you can work out how to respond.

I urge parents to listen to their children. I urge schoolteachers, counselors, attorneys ad litem and amicus attorneys, law enforcement, and CPS workers to listen to the children. People of integrity who love the children and who love justice need to listen to what these children are saying.

Unfortunately, there are sexual predators among us as we move through our daily lives. We just don't know who they are because we assume that the "bad people" are locked up in jail, giving us a deceptive sense of safety. A few months ago, I was at the grocery store, and I looked up to see Jay, my client's ex-husband, standing in the checkout line to pay for his groceries.

I have read the thousands of pages of evidence from counseling notes and law enforcement investigations that indicate he has sexually abused his children and sex trafficked them, and they have reported and described the murders he has committed. It was a very good reminder that there are all kinds of people moving among us. I know what his children have said about him. I know the details of the description his sons gave as they described him shooting and killing little Joy and Josh in Oklahoma. I believe his children, even if he testifies on the witness stand that everything they say is a lie. I call for justice for his two sons. I call for justice for Joy and Josh. I call for justice for all those he harmed.

Listen to the children.

PUZZLE PIECES

- What do you think about Dr. Vo's testimony in Janice's case? Does she seem to understand how children process and exhibit things like trauma and abuse?
- When she says children cannot fake emotion, what does she mean by that?

- In the exhibit, Dr. Vo lists several things parents and caregivers can do to help children who have been abused. Is there anything you can use with your own children to help them become more articulate and self-aware?
- What is your biggest takeaway from the cases you have read?
- Have you been able to notice patterns, connecting pieces in the puzzle that Attorney Clack has presented in this book? If so, what are they?

Epilogue

THE BILLION-DOLLAR BATTLE

According to a report filed by the White House in 2021, the perpetrators of sex trafficking are responsible for an estimated $150 billion annually in illicit profits.[1]

When I was thinking about what to write for the final chapter of this book, I had the idea to reach out to someone I know who possesses extensive knowledge about sex trafficking in West Texas. I thought it would be a perfect opportunity for this woman, for whom I have tremendous admiration, to talk about her work and experiences with trying to help victims of sex trafficking.

She speaks to local organizations and presents compelling programs. She travels around the United States and trains law enforcement officers and others on how to deal with sex trafficking. Although we have been discussing this for months, I learned that she didn't feel like she could contribute anything to this book without the approval of the board of directors of her organization. I have since heard that she is declining to contribute.

Obviously, we as a nation and as a society have a huge mountain to climb if we are going to help the victims of sex trafficking. We need a whole lot of light to shine on a vast amount of darkness to reveal the predators and the people who protect the predators. We need people of integrity and courage to speak out and do their job to help the victims of these crimes and activities.

As I write this, I understand the story will never be finished. There are so many people out there who have stories of their own. There are women and men, victims of sexual abuse, who are now in their fifties, sixties, and seventies who have remained silent because they thought no one cared or that no one would believe them.

When I have spoken at a meeting regarding the subject matter of sexual abuse of children, women have come forward to share with me their own stories of childhood abuse and how a sibling was abused by a family member. These women were crying as they described things that happened fifty or sixty years ago.

I know there are thousands of others who have suffered greatly from sexual abuse in their childhood and those who are survivors of child sex trafficking. There are thousands of people who are survivors who have not been listened to and have not been believed. Many of these victims and survivors have had their voices ignored and silenced by the ignorance of the listener and, yes, even by the people who operate in some sort of organized effort to protect the predators.

Maybe not all of these predators and their protectors are participating in ritualistic abuse, but they are still operating together to cover up vile acts of sexual abuse, either by turning a blind eye of inaction or by actively assisting to proclaim the victims and survivors as liars. They use tactics of fear and shame to keep the survivors silent.

This is truly a battle of good versus evil. If the statistics are correct and this is a $150 billion business, then there are many more people involved in this organized crime of child sex trafficking than the cases I have shared with you in this book.

What is your answer to this call for justice? Will you be courageous enough to help shine the light?

NOTES

INTRODUCTION

1. ILO et al., *Global Estimates of Modern Slavery: Forced Labour and Forced Marriage* (September 2022), https://www.ilo.org/sites/default/files/2025-09/ILO_GEMS-2022_Report_EN_Web.pdf.

2. Russell Gold, "The Billionaire Bully Who Wants to Turn Texas into a Christian Theocracy," *Texas Monthly* (March 2024), https://www.texasmonthly.com/news-politics/billionaire-tim-dunn-runs-texas/.

3. Stewart Doreen, "Report: Midland Ranks as Texas' Wealthiest County," *Midland-Reporter Telegram*, June 20, 2022, https://www.mrt.com/news/local/article/Report-Midland-ranks-as-Texas-wealthiest-county-17253931.php.

4. City of Midland, "BEA: Midland Ranks 2nd in US in Per Capita Personal Income by Metro Area," news release, November 15, 2024, https://www.midlandtexas.gov/CivicAlerts.aspx?AID=1594.

CHAPTER 1

1. "Statistics: Victims of Sexual Violence," RAINN, updated August 18, 2025, https://rainn.org/facts-statistics-the-scope-of-the-problem/statistics-victims-of-sexual-violence/.

2. "Judge Dean Rucker," Midland County Staff Directory, accessed January 26, 2026. https://www.co.midland.tx.us/Directory.aspx?EID=132.

CHAPTER 2

1. Cassandra Wiener et al., "A State of Siege: How Abusers Leverage Fear and Control," Bhekisisa Centre for Health Journalism, February 17, 2022, https://bhekisisa.org/article/2022-02-17-a-state-of-siege-how-abusers-leverage-fear-and-control/.

CHAPTER 3

1. Lindsay Malloy et al., "Filial Dependency and Recantation of Child Sexual Abuse Allegations," *Journal of the American Academy of Child & Adolescent Psychiatry* 46, no. 2 (March 2007): 162–170, https://www.researchgate.net/publication/6559748_Filial_Dependency_and_Recantation_of_Child_Sexual_Abuse_Allegations.

CHAPTER 4

1. Joan Meier et al., "Child Custody Outcomes in Cases Involving Parental Alienation and Abuse Allegations," GWU Law School Public Law Research Paper No. 2019-56, 2019, https://scholarship.law.gwu.edu/cgi/viewcontent.cgi?article=2712&context=faculty_publications.

CHAPTER 5

1. Karen Oehme and Sharon Maxwell, "Six Crucial Issues in Supervised Visitation," US Department of Justice, September 2004, https://www.ojp.gov/pdffiles1/Archive/221748NCJRS.pdf.
2. Centers for Children and Families, LinkedIn, accessed February 4, 2026, https://www.linkedin.com/company/centers-for-children-and-families/; Centers for Children and Families, United Way of Midland, accessed February 4, 2026, https://www.uwmidland.org/centers-children-and-families.
3. Centers for Children and Families, Inc., Bizapedia.com, Company Information Search, accessed February 4, 2026, https://www.bizapedia.com/tx/centers-for-children-and-families-inc.html.
4. "318th Family District County," Midland County, TX, accessed February 4, 2026, https://www.co.midland.tx.us/288/318th-Family-District-Court.

CHAPTER 6

1. Jennifer Harman et al., "Gender and Child Custody Outcomes Across 16 Years of Judicial Decisions Regarding Abuse and Parental Alienation," *Children and Youth Services Review* 155 (2023): 107187, https://www.sciencedirect.com/science/article/pii/S0190740923003833?via%3Dihub.VERSION-OF-HARMAN-LUDMER-ARTICLE.pdf.

CHAPTER 7

1. ILO et al., *Global Estimates of Modern Slavery.*

CHAPTER 8

1. Katarina Herring-Trott, "Bastions of Independence or Shields of Misconduct?: Increasing Transparency in Judicial Conduct Commissions," *Fordham Law Review* 92, no. 2 (2023), https://ir.lawnet.fordham.edu/cgi/viewcontent.cgi?article=6043&context=flr.

CHAPTER 9

1. Billy Binion, "For 20 Years, This Prosecutor Had a Secret Job Working for the Judges Who'd Decide His Cases," *US Observer* 2, no. 63 (May 3, 2022), https://usobserver.com/wp-content/uploads/2022/05/usobserver-may-22-num63-vWEB.pdf.
2. State Bar of Texas, "Miscellaneous Documents," *Texas Bar Journal* 84, no. 6 (June 2021): 544–69, https://www.texasbar.com/AM/Template.cfm?Section=Home&ContentID=53510&Template=/CM/ContentDisplay.cfm.
3. Jessica Priest, "Moonlighting Prosecutor Sent Texas Man to Death Row; 17 Years Later, He Could Get a New Trial," *USA Today*, February 4, 2021, https://www.usatoday.com/in-depth/news/investigations/2021/02/04/texas-death-row-inmate-could-get-new-trial/4255647001/.
4. Alexa Gervasi and Daryl James, "When Civil Immunity Becomes Impunity," *The Wall Street Journal*, April 11, 2022, https://www.wsj.com/opinion/civil-immunity-ralph-petty-disbarred-corrupt-lawsuit-judge-law-court-west-midland-texas-civil-rights-11649706400?mod=Searchresults&pos=2&paqe=1.

5. "Midland Prosecutor," Institute for Justice, https://ij.org/case/midland-prosecutor/.

6. Roxanna Asgarian, "Moonlighting Texas Prosecutor Sued," *Texas Observer*, September 19, 2023, https://www.texasobserver.org/clinton-young-death-row-lawsuit-midland/.

7. Stewart Doreen, "Lawsuit Filed Against Midland County, Former ADA Ralph Petty," *Midland Reporter-Telegram*, April 12, 2022, https://www.mrt.com/news/local/article/Lawsuit-filed-against-Midland-County-former-ADA-17076338.php.

8. "Clinton Young Files Lawsuit Against Midland County, Ralph Petty and Former Midland County District Attorneys," NewsWest9, September 20, 2023, https://www.newswest9.com/article/news/local/clinton-young-files-lawsuit-against-midland-county-ralph-petty-and-former-midland-county-district-attorneys/513-7c84f3e0-284b-4cef-a27c-11abc198d4e7.

9. Jack Marshall, "Ralph Petty, the Moonlighting Texas ADA, Strikes Again!" *Ethics Alarms* (blog), January 20, 2024, https://ethicsalarms.com/2024/01/20/ralph-petty-the-moonlighting-texas-ada-strikes-again/.

10. Jack Marshall, "A Scandal That Compels the Question: If This Can Happen, What Other Ethics Rot Lurks in the Justice System?" *Ethics Alarms* (blog), May 17, 2021, https://ethicsalarms.com/2021/05/17/a-scandal-that-compels-the-question-if-this-can-happen-what-other-ethics-rot-lurks-in-the-justice-system/.

CHAPTER 10

1. Casey Brown et al., *Child Physical Abuse and Neglect* (StatPearls Publishing, 2023).

CHAPTER 11

1. Becki Goggins and Anne Gallegos, "State Progress in Record Reporting for Firearm-Related Background Checks: Protection Order Submissions," Bureau of Justice Statistics, April 2016, https://www.ojp.gov/pdffiles1/bjs/grants/249864.pdf.

CHAPTER 12

1. Mark Motivans and Tracey Kyckelhahn, "Federal Prosecution of Child Sex Exploitation Offenders, 2006," Bureau of Justice Statistics, December 2007, https://bjs.ojp.gov/content/pub/pdf/fpcseo06.pdf.
2. Brian Rogers, "Odessa Police Chief Retires," *Odessa American*, September 14, 2001, https://oaoa.newspapers.com/search/results/?date-end=2002&date-start=2001&keyword=Odessa+police+chief+retires&publication-ids=1328.
3. Dean Stephens, "Deputy Police Chief Refutes Allegations," *Odessa American*, April 13, 1993, https://oaoa.newspapers.com/image/300740151/?match=1&terms=Deputy%20police%20chief%20refutes%20allegations; Dean Sueltenfuss, "Police Officials Suite Dismissed," *Odessa American*, May 19, 1993, https://oaoa.newspapers.com/search/results/?date-end=1994&date-start=1993&keyword=Police+official%27s+suit+dismissed&publication-ids=1328.
4. USA v. Jenkins, No. 7:01-cr-00106-RAJ-1, (Western District of Texas [Midland], September 14, 2001), ECF No. 8–10.
5. Brian Rogers, "Ex-Chief Pleads Guilty to Child Porn," *Odessa American*, September 15, 2001, https://oaoa.newspapers.com/newspage/301728621/.
6. "Top 10 of 2001," *Odessa American*, January 1, 2002, https://oaoa.newsbank.com/sign-up?docref=doc/news/111236E7AA066BD6%3Fsearch_terms%3Dtop%2Bstories%2B2001%26date_from%3D1999%26date_to%3D2006%26text%3Dtop.

CHAPTER 13

1. Texas Department of Family and Protective Services, *Fiscal Year 2024 Child Maltreatment Fatalities and Near Fatalities Annual Report*, 2025, https://www.dfps.texas.gov/About_DFPS/Reports_and_Presentations/Office_of_Child_Safety/documents/child-fatality-reports/2025-03-05_Child_Maltreatment_Fatalities_and_Near_Fatalities_Annual_Report.pdf; TexProtects, "Child Abuse and Neglect Risks During COVID-19," 2020, https://tex.3dev.co/wp-content/uploads/2022/04/child_abuse_and_neglect_risk_during_covid-19.pdf.

CHAPTER 14

1. Danielle Pollack, "Statistics on Child Abuse/Child Sexual Abuse and the Family Courts," Child USA, 2019, https://childusa.org/wp-content/uploads/2020/03/StatisticsonChildAbuseintheCourtw.pdf.

CHAPTER 15

1. Children's Bureau of the US Department of Health and Human Services, *Child Maltreatment 2022*, 2024, https://acf.gov/sites/default/files/documents/cb/cm2022.pdf.

CHAPTER 16

1. Children's Bureau of the US Department of Health and Human Services, *Child Maltreatment 2022*.
2. Texas Family Code, art. 261, sec. 101, https://statutes.capitol.texas.gov/?tab=1&code=FA&chapter=FA.261&artSec=261.101.
3. "1260 Administrative Review of Investigation Findings," Texas Department of Family and Protective Services, accessed February 4, 2026, https://www.dfps.texas.gov/handbooks/cps/files/CPS_pg_1260.asp.

CHAPTER 17

1. Andrew Ortiz, *Delayed Disclosure: Child USA 2024 Factsheet*, Child USA, 2024, https://childusa.org/wp-content/uploads/2024/06/Delayed-Disclosure-2024.pdf.

EPILOGUE

1. The White House, "Fact Sheet: The National Action Plan to Combat Human Trafficking (NAP)," release, December 3, 2021, https://bidenwhitehouse.archives.gov/briefing-room/statements-releases/2021/12/03/fact-sheet-the-national-action-plan-to-combat-human-trafficking-nap/.

ABOUT THE AUTHOR

Author photography by Diana Taylor Burge and Halstan Williams

With a Texas Supreme Court justice, a state district judge, and three more attorneys in the family, Cynthia L. Clack has an inside track in Texas courtrooms and a passion for impossible cases.

Cynthia was admitted to the State Bar of Texas in 1978, becoming only the third woman to practice law in the West Texas city of Odessa. To get her solo practice off the ground, Cynthia served as a part-time municipal judge and a city attorney and taught business law at the local community college.

She now serves clients throughout Texas, the United States, and internationally in divorce, child custody, child abuse, and other family law matters, as well as catastrophic personal injury lawsuits.

Her advocacy for underdog clients has resulted in victories in high-dollar child custody trials, the acquittal of a man who confessed to a horrific murder that he did not commit, and the resolution of an international kidnapping case that made Cynthia and her client, Emily Wu, celebrities in China. Cynthia is certified by the Texas Board of Legal Specialization in family law, and she is a mediator, but it is her extrajudicial work that connects her with people from all walks of life.

Cynthia wrote the libretto and song lyrics for the 2005 rock opera *Eye of the Tiger*, performed at Odessa's Globe of the Great Southwest Theater. She wrote and published *Doodles the American Poodle*, a series of books for children of US servicemen and women, as well as a memoir, *The Other Side of Life—An Angel's Story*. She teaches an office-management seminar for attorneys and their staff and is a sought-after public speaker.

She has served as a member of multiple boards and community service organizations, including the Goodwill West Texas board of directors, the board of directors of the Midland–Odessa Symphony and Chorale, the Baylor Law Alumni Executive Committee, and the Advisory Council for Texas Tech University Health Sciences Center.

Cynthia graduated from Baylor University School of Law in Waco, Texas, in 1978. Her late father, James H. Clack, served as a Texas district judge. Her late mother, Knoxine Campbell Clack, taught school in Texas independent school districts for over thirty years. Cynthia's late stepmother, Barbara Culver Clack, was the second woman appointed to the Texas Supreme Court. Her brother Steve is a Texas-based attorney, as was her late brother Gene. Cynthia lives and works in Odessa, Texas.

www.ingramcontent.com/pod-product-compliance
Lightning Source LLC
Chambersburg PA
CBHW031341230926
51848CB00002B/327
* 9 7 8 1 9 6 6 6 2 9 7 7 1 *